Beginning Bobbin Lace

Beginning Bobbin Lace

GILIAN DYE

Dover Publications, Inc., New York

With thanks to all my lacemaking friends in the North East for their help and encouragement, in particular to my students, old and young, who have tried out patterns, and refuelled my enthusiasm with their pleasure in discovering the fascination of bobbin lace.

Photography by David Bradwell.

Library of Congress Cataloging-in-Publication Data

Dye, Gilian.
    Beginning bobbin lace.

    (Dover needlework series)
    Reprint. Originally published: London : Dryad Press, 1986.
    Bibliography: p.
    Includes index.
    1. Bobbin lace.   I. Title.   II. Series.
[TT805.D929   1987]   746.2'22   86-24121
ISBN 0-486-25416-X

Contents

Abbreviations

w.st. – whole stitch (cr., tw., cr.)

$\frac{1}{2}$st. – half stitch (cr., tw.)

dbl – double (cr., tw., cr., tw.)

pr(s) – pair(s) of bobbins or threads

wks – workers

cr. – cross (left over right from one pair to another)

tw. – twist (right over left within a pair)

Introduction

Bobbin lace is an open fabric made by the twisting of numerous threads. Exactly how, when and where the craft was invented is impossible to say. It probably developed from the plaiting of fringes on woven fabrics, and was certainly practised in the sixteenth century. By the 1650s it was both an art form and a thriving industry with centres in Italy, Flanders, France and England.

Once machine lace was perfected (around 1840) it was no longer possible for any but the most expert hand-worker to make a living from lacemaking and the craft declined rapidly, reaching an all time low in the first half of this century. However the 1960s and 1970s saw the beginning of a lacemaking revival, not this time as a commercial proposition, but as a rewarding and challenging hobby now enjoyed by many thousands of people of all ages.

This book sets out to provide step by step instructions for the complete beginner who might be working on her (or his) own. With lacemaking, as with any other craft, it is easier to learn from an enthusiastic teacher than entirely from the pages of a book. If you can get to one of the many evening (or day) classes, or a weekend course, then use this as a reference book and source of ideas. If not, then work through the detailed projects which will give you practice in all the basic lacemaking techniques.

Most patterns are open to many interpretations. The sections headed 'Variations' show ways in which the pieces can be adapted using different threads and/or techniques, or by modifying the pricking in some way.

1
Equipment

The techniques of bobbin lace are somewhere between those of plaiting and weaving. Any number of *threads* may be used – from around a dozen to a thousand or more. For convenience the threads are wound on short handles called *bobbins*. The lace is worked over a pattern, called a *pricking*, which is fixed on a firm *pillow*. As the lace is formed the threads are held in position by *pins* stuck through holes in the pricking and into the pillow.

The essentials for beginning bobbin lace are described here and

Fig. 1. Lacemaking equipment: pins and pin cushion; various threads (Fils à Dentelles, coton perle, Brillante d'Alsace, sewing cotton, linen, metallic yarns); crochet hooks; pricker and square of beeswax; bobbins; bobbin holder; all on a sheet of pricking card

illustrated in Figs. 1–4. As you become more involved with the craft you will gradually extend your stock of equipment – details of other useful items can be found in chapter 6.

Thread

Almost any yarn can be used for making lace. Traditionally most of the best lace was made from ecru or white linen, but silk (often black) and cotton were also used. Today we also have a wide range of synthetic fibres and mixtures which will give original results. The threads for each project are given in the instructions – if the named thread is not available use a thread of similar thickness (a table of comparison is given in Fig. 79). No. 8 coton perle and an oddment of DK wool will carry you through chapter 2, with a finer thread such as Fils à Dentelles required in chapter 3.

Bobbins

There are many types of bobbin (see Figs. 1 and 81). Most are about 10cm (4in.) long, all have a head, a neck on which the thread is wound and a handle (Fig. 2). Some have a little ring of beads, called a *spangle*, which adds weight and prevents the bobbin from rolling about on the pillow. Spangles help to keep an even tension when working a length of lace, but are a nuisance when making lace that requires many 'sewings' (see chapter 4). Antique bobbins although lovely to have and to work with do the job no better than inexpensive plastic or dowelling bobbins (readily available by mail order).

Start with about 12 pairs – i.e. 24 bobbins – but be prepared to add more for some of the pieces described.

Pillow

Lace pillows come in many shapes and sizes (see Fig. 80). The traditional filling is tightly packed straw, but polystyrene is often used today.

For a practice pillow you need a block of polystyrene about 45cm (18in.) square and 3.5cm (1½in.) thick. Use packing material or several large ceiling tiles. Round the corners and slope the edges of the block using a large knife heated in boiling water, leave a smooth top surface. Cover the surface with one or two layers of felt, then enclose the whole pillow in a smooth

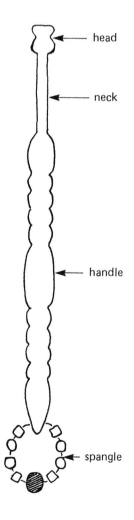

Fig. 2. An English ('Bucks') bobbin with bead spangle

head

neck

handle

spangle

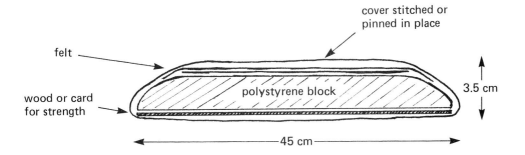

Fig. 3. Polystyrene pillow

(preferably dark coloured) fabric such as sheeting. Thick card or thin wood under the polystyrene will reduce the risk of breakage (Fig. 3).

Pins

Ordinary dressmaking pins are quite suitable as a start, but for finer work you will need brass lace pins. Keep the pins handy in a small, fluff-free (not felt) pin cushion.

Prickings

Patterns were once pricked on parchment, these days glazed card is used. If you are unable to obtain a sheet of the special pricking card use any strong smooth card, or architects' tracing film (see chapter 6). For making holes in the pricking you will need a pricker, this is a fine needle held in a handle of some kind (a cork, block of wood or pin-vice) (Fig. 4). A block of beeswax (or a candle) is useful for lubricating the needle.

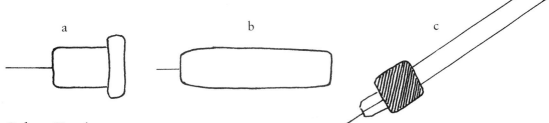

Fig. 4. Prickers, needle held in a) Cork b) Wood block c) Pin-vice

Other Equipment

Two pieces of fabric as cover-cloths: one approximately 45cm × 30cm (18in. × 12in.); the other 45cm × 45cm (18in. × 18in.) – this larger cloth is to cover the pillow at all times when it is not in use. Small *sharp* scissors; fine crochet hooks (1.00 and 0.60) and sewing needles.

For making the prickings: tracing paper; pencil; rubber; ruler; sticky tape; ballpoint (or fibretip) pen; scissors.

2
Basic Stitches

Plait

Even when managing a pillow with a hundred or more bobbins you will still handle only two prs at a time. Working a 4-strand plait will give you the feel of the bobbins and of the two movements, the *cross* (cr.) and the *twist* (tw.), which make most lace stitches.

Preparation
Wind 4 bobbins with No. 8 coton perle.
Winding a bobbin
Make a slip knot at the end of a thread and insert the bobbin (Fig. 5a); wind the thread clockwise using the whole length of the neck

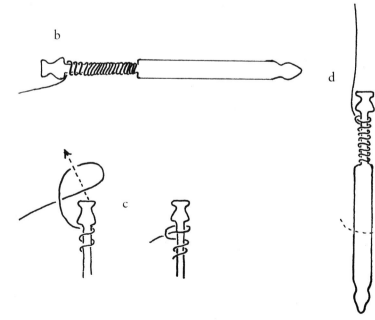

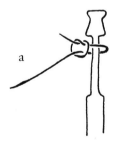

Fig. 5. Winding a bobbin
a) starting with a slip knot
b) winding c) hitch to secure
thread d) lengthening the
thread

– one or two layers are sufficient for samples, for larger pieces the neck can be filled completely, (Fig. 5b); finish with a hitch (Fig. 5c).

Let the bobbin hang from the thread – it should not unwind, if it does then try the hitch again. Still holding the thread try a clockwise turn on the bobbin (Fig. 5d) – this should lengthen the free thread.

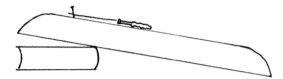

Fig. 6. Position of pillow

Tilt the pillow slightly by resting it on a book. Knot the four threads together and pin, through the knot, to the top of the pillow (Fig. 6). Release the thread, or rewind, as required until all the bobbins are the same distance from the pin – approximately 12cm (5in.).

Working a plait
Take a pr of bobbins in each hand:
Cross the inside bobbin of the left-hand pr over the inside bobbin of the right-hand pr (Fig. 7a); then *twist* each pr by taking the right-hand bobbin over the left of the same pr (Fig. 7b). Repeat the *cross* and *twist* until you no longer need to think about the movements. The plait you produce, (Fig. 8), will probably be

Fig. 7. a) Cross b) cross followed by twist or both pairs

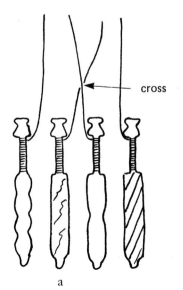

cross

a

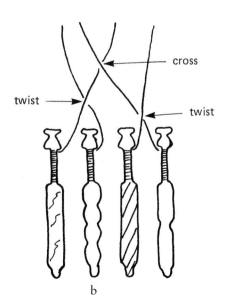

cross

twist

twist

b

Fig. 8. Plait

fairly loose, it can be tightened by pulling the two prs apart at intervals.

Wherever they come in a piece of lace the cr. is *always* left over right and the tw. right over left. Two prs are usually twisted at the same time.

Variations
Work this 4-strand plait with strips of material (folded and stitched) as a belt, dress trim or hair band.

Sampler of Stitches

The three basic lacemaking stitches are *whole stitch* (sometimes called cloth stitch), *double stitch* (cloth stitch and twist) and *half stitch* (Fig. 9). To work a sampler of these stitches you will need a pricking taken from Pricking 1 and 14 bobbins wound with No.8 coton perle.

Preparation
Make a pricking on a strip of card approximately 3cm × 25cm (1¼in. × 10in.):

a) Trace (or photocopy) the pattern taking particular care with the position of dots (pin-holes); fix the tracing to one end of the pricking card with sticky tape; place card on a pad of material or the back of a cork mat; using a pricker held as upright as possible, prick through each pin-hole.

b) Move the traced pattern down the card positioning the first few holes on the tracing over the last few on the card; fix in position and prick, omitting holes *B*, *C* and *D* (Fig. 10).

c) Remove the tracing and copy all the markings on to the card using a fine ball-point or fibre-tip pen.

This is the general method for making any pricking, stage b) is obviously omitted for any complete pattern, e.g. motif or bookmark.

Set up the pillow with the pricking down the centre, lettered holes at the top (Fig. 11). Cover the lower part of the pricking and pillow with a small cover cloth. Wind the bobbins as described above. Knot together the threads from 1 pr of bobbins and pin through the knot, at *A* – these will be the *workers* (wks). Knot and pin 2 prs at each of *B*, *C* and *D* – these 6 prs will be *passives*. Adjust the length of thread between pin and bobbin until all the bobbins lie on the cover cloth. Place pins handy in a small pin cushion.

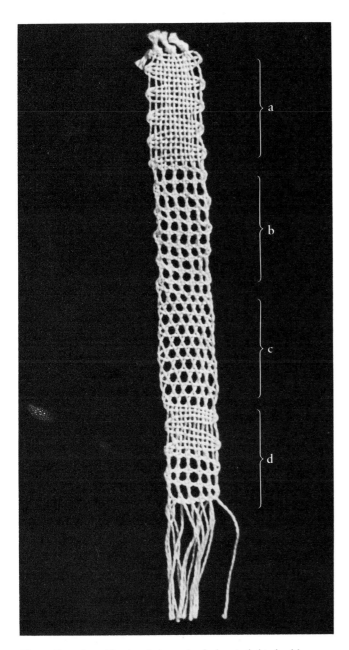

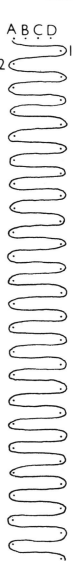

Fig. 9. Sampler of basic stitches: a) whole stitch b) doubles
c) half stitch d) whole stitch and doubles

Pricking 1. Stitch sampler

Whole stitch

Whole stitch, abbreviated as *w.st* is shown in Fig. 9a.

Pick up the wks (from *A*) in your left hand and the 1st pr of
passives (from *B*) in your right and work a w.st.: *cross inside*

Fig. 10. Making a pricking

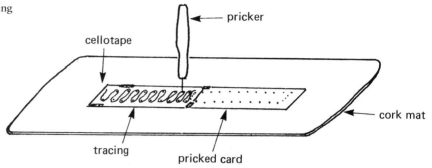

Fig. 11. Setting up the pillow

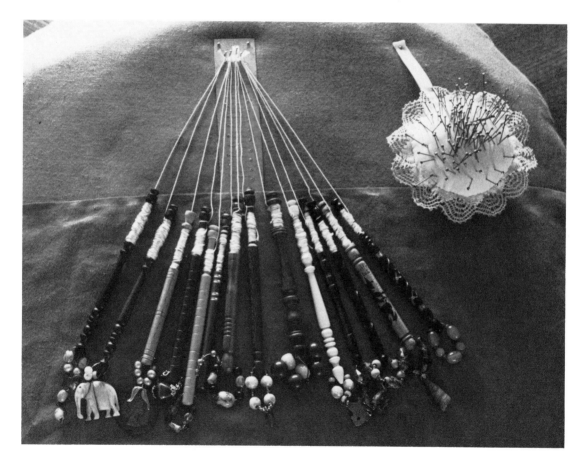

threads, *twist both pairs, cross inside threads again* (this can be abbreviated as *cr., tw., cr.*). See Fig. 12a.

* The passives will now be in your left hand, push these to the side, transfer the wks to your left hand and pick up the next pr of passives in your right. Work a w.st. (*cr., tw., cr.*) with these 2 prs. Repeat from * to the end of the row, 6 w.st. altogether. Insert a pin

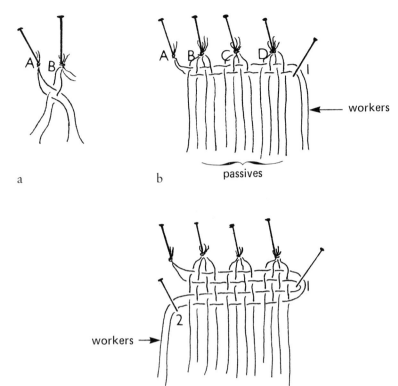

Fig. 12. Whole stitch: a) one stitch b) one row c) two rows

at 1 between the wks and the last pr of passives – angle the pin so the head is slightly behind and to the side of the point (Fig. 12b).

Work back across the passives with 6 w.st. This time the wks will be in your right hand at the start of each stitch, but the cr. is still left over right and the tw. right over left. Put in a pin at 2, between wks and passives (Fig. 12c).

Work from side to side for 10 to 12 rows (or until you can make a w.st. without really thinking). If the passives are bunched up at the end of the row they can be straightened, after putting in the pin, by pulling their bobbins with one hand while holding the wks with the other. However, it is better practice, and a good deal quicker, to give any necessary pull while working the return row. Finish with the wks on the left ready to start a section of doubles.

Doubles

A double (*dbl*), shown in Fig. 9b, has one more movement than a w.st. Using the 2 left-hand prs, work the 1st dbl: *cross, twist both pairs, cross, twist both pairs* (i.e. *cr., tw., cr., tw.*). See Fig. 13a.

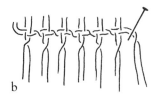

a

b

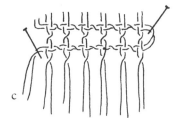

c

Fig. 13. Doubles: a) one stitch b) one row c) two rows

Work 5 more dbls across the row, putting the passives to the side after each stitch, and pin between the last 2 prs (Fig. 13b). Then work from side to side, as for the w.st. (Fig. 13c). NB At the start of the 2nd, and subsequent rows, all prs have one tw. Passives may need a firm pull. Finish on the left.

Half stitch
A half stitch ($\frac{1}{2}$st.), shown in Fig. 9c, has only 2 movements so the prs do not stay together as wks and passives.
Again starting with the 2 left-hand prs: *cross, twist both pairs* (i.e. *cr., tw.*) (Fig. 14a).

a

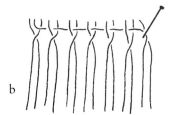

b

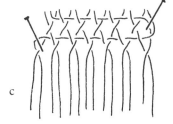

c

Fig. 14. Half stitch: a) one stitch b) one row c) two rows

After the 1st $\frac{1}{2}$st. push the 2 bobbins, now in the left hand, to the side in the usual way and pick up the next pr. Work 5 more $\frac{1}{2}$st., pin (Fig. 14b), then work from side to side with 6 $\frac{1}{2}$st. on each row (Fig. 14c).
Remind yourself of w.st. and dbls by working a few rows of each (Fig. 9d), before cutting threads a few centimetres from the end of the sampler. Remove the pins carefully.

Variations
Use 2 or more colours, or thicknesses of yarn.
Try the effect of: extra tws. between stitches; working different

stitches on the same row; alternate rows of different stitches; etc.
Also see chapter 4 – Braids.

Working notes

You have now mastered the basics of lacemaking. The following
notes should help you to make the most of your efforts, and will
perhaps answer some of the questions that have already occurred
to you.

1. Don't look at the bobbins while you work – look at the
threads.
2. Handle the threads as little as possible.
3. Always cover the pillow when it is not in use.
4. Push pins about halfway in, sloping them slightly so the heads
are away from you and out from the edge of your work – this
keeps a firm edge on your lace, stops it lifting off the pricking and
allows you to see what you are doing (Fig. 15).
5. Pins can be removed from the back of the work when they are
no longer needed to resist the pull on any bobbin – e.g. pins *1* and
2 can be removed before *B* or *C*.
6. If you notice a mistake in your work then it is usually worth
putting it right, this is a matter of retracing your steps and
working each stage in reverse. If you watch the threads, not the
bobbins, you should find it quite straightforward, if rather
tedious, to work back to the error. Do not remove the pins until
you reach them (or the work will collapse on itself). Once the
error has been removed check before continuing that all the
bobbins are in the correct position, with threads twisted where
necessary.
7. When you need to move your pillow fix the bobbins down in
one of the following ways:

   a) put the heads of bobbins into a crochet bobbin holder (see p.
   90), pin the holder to the pillow (Fig. 16a);
   b) turn the small cover cloth over the bobbins and pin through
   both layers, trapping the working threads in correct order, pin
   the cloth to the pillow (Fig. 16b);
   c) put a bandage, or length of elastic across the pillow and pin
   firmly between the bobbins (Fig. 16c).

8. If you run out of thread on any bobbin a new length can be
added as follows: remove the bobbin from the work and wind on
fresh thread; tie the new end to the last pin worked by that
bobbin; tuck the old end of the thread under the hitch before
pulling it tight (Fig. 17a); work with this double thread until the

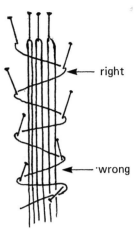

right

wrong

Fig. 15. Angle of pins

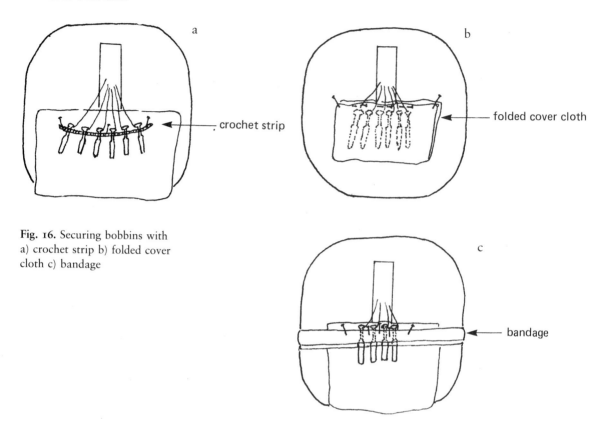

Fig. 16. Securing bobbins with
a) crochet strip b) folded cover
cloth c) bandage

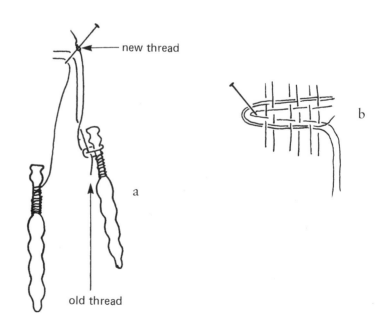

Fig. 17. Joining threads

new thread is locked in place (Fig. 17b); when the pins are removed, trim the ends close. Towards the end of a piece, a worker that is running out can often be exchanged for a passive by putting in an extra tw. or cr. (Fig. 18).

9. When your work reaches the end of the pricking move it back to the start as follows: put the bobbins into a bobbin holder (Fig. 16a), or cover cloth (Fig. 16b), and support their weight with one hand; carefully remove all pins; move the work up and repin the last few centimetres to the top of the pricking, matching the pattern where necessary and being careful not to pull on any bobbin while the threads are unpinned (Fig. 19); release the bobbins, check their positions and continue with the work.

10. On a polystyrene pillow the pricking should be moved slightly each time it is used so the pins do not go into the same place.

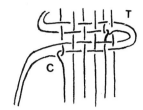

Fig. 18. Exchanging passives for workers: C – with a cross; T – with a twist

Fig. 19. Moving work – note slackness of threads between lace and bobbins while pins are replaced

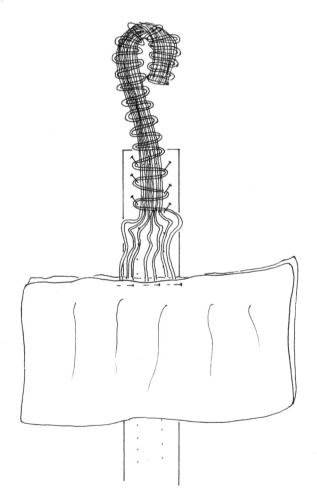

11. It is almost impossible to estimate the amount of yarn needed for any piece. Wks going from side to side obviously use up much more than passives which just run along the length, however, in many laces the threads constantly change direction. Do not over fill your bobbins, this just soils the yarn and prevents the hitch from holding. If you run out of thread make a join as described in 8. (page 19) – Fig. 17. Oddments of yarn left on bobbins can be used for mounting or to try out new stitches. Putting a measured amount on each bobbin is not usually a good idea – joins would tend to come all at once (the only sample for which a measurement is given is the flower head below, which uses very little thread).

Flower (Fig. 20)

This design gives further practice in the three basic stitches and introduces different methods of starting and finishing.

Make separate prickings from Pricking 2 for the flower, stem and leaf.

Flower head (Pricking 2a)

Pin the flower pricking to the centre of your pillow, lettered holes on the right; cover the lower pricking with a cloth. Wind 1 pr of bobbins with DK wool (these will be the wks), and 6 prs with No. 8 coton perle (passives). For this 75 cm (30 in.) of thread for each pr

Pricking 2. Flower: a) flower head b) stem c) leaf

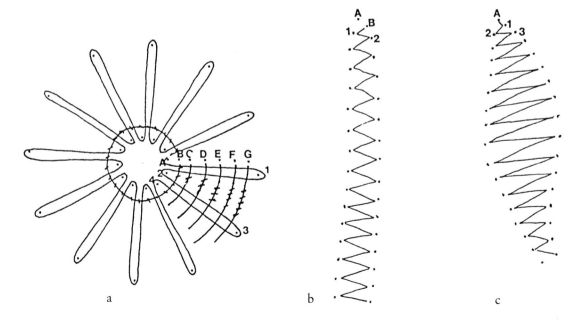

a   b   c

Fig. 20. Flower

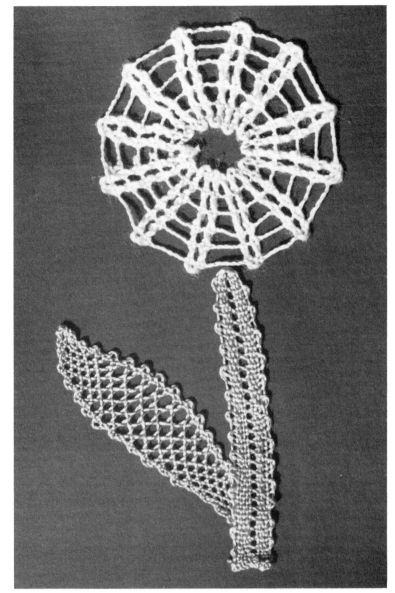

Fig. 21. Bobbins wound as a
pair

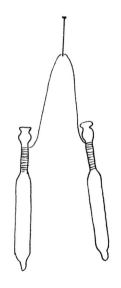

of passives and 2m (80in.) for the wks will be ample. The bobbins
should be *wound in prs*: wind one bobbin in the normal way;
unwind more yarn from the ball, cut: wind 2nd bobbin from this
end (Fig. 21). Almost all patterns require that the bobbins are
wound in this way – it is much neater and halves the number of
ends to be dealt with (you may find that the threads slip about a
bit at the start, be patient it gets better – as a last resort put a tw.
about the pin, or in the case of a thick yarn, put the pin through
the thread).

Hang wks at *A* and 1 pr of passives at each of *B* to *G*. * Starting with the wks in the left hand, work a dbl with each pr of passives (the wks should now be on the right). Put in a pin at *1*. Work back to the centre with another 6 dbls (on this row the wks will be in the right hand at the start of each stitch). Pin at *2*. Leave the wks while you make extra tws. in the passives as indicated by ₩ on the pricking – each pr will already be twisted once (or should be after a dbl!), so put 4 extra tws. in the outside pr, 3 in the next, etc. Repeat from * all round.

Turn the pillow, and move the cover cloth, at intervals so the work is always coming towards you. After a few rows the pins can be pushed right down so they do not catch on the threads, or your fingers, but do not do this too soon or the wks will slip over the pin heads.

When the circle is complete – i.e. when the wks are again at *A* and the passives have all their tws. – finish off as follows:
1. Remove the pin from *A*.
2. Put a fine crochet hook through the loop where the pin was and pull through one of the wks (Fig. 22a).
3. Pass the other bobbin of the pr through the loop thus formed (Fig. 22b).
4. Pull threads tight (Fig. 22c).

a

b

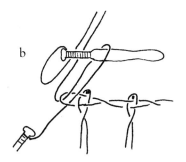

c

d

Fig. 22. Finishing the flower head: a–c) making a sewing d) reef knot (i) first half, (ii) complete knot

i   ii

5. Tie a firm reef knot with the 2 threads (Fig. 22d).

6. Replace the pin.

Repeat stages 1–6 with each pr of passives taking each to the appropriate starting pin. Cut the threads close to the knots. Carefully remove all pins. (The knots can be sealed with a spot of transparent glue.)

Stages 1–4 make up the technique known as a 'sewing'.

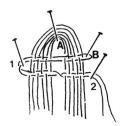

Fig. 23. Starting the stem

Stem (Pricking 2b)

Pin the pricking with the point towards the top of your pillow. Wind 7 prs with No. 8 coton perle, hang 6 of the prs (passives) over a pin at A, the 7th pr (wks) at B. Work across all the passives in w.st., pin at *1*. * Work back across the stem with: tw. wks, 3 w.st., tw. wks, 3 w.st., pin (at 2), see Fig. 23. Repeat from * to end of stem.

Finish with the type of knotted finish used in Bruges lace (Fig. 24, see page 26): tie a reef knot with the 2 right-hand threads; * push the bobbin now in the left hand under the right hand, pick up the next bobbin along, tie *half* a reef with this; repeat from * to last pr, tie a complete reef with these. Working now from left to right and dropping the right-hand bobbin each time, work the 2nd half of the knots, finishing with a complete knot on the right. All knots should be pulled tight – if you overdo it and snap a thread don't worry, it should be trapped and held by the knots on either side. Cut the threads close and remove pins.

Leaf (Pricking 2c)

Wind 7 prs with No. 8 coton perle. Hang 4 prs across the pricking at A. Tw. the 2 prs on the left, dbl with the 2 right-hand prs, pin at *1* (Fig. 25a). Dbl (with right-hand prs) then work to the left with ½st., dbl, pin at 2, dbl.

Hang a new pr on 2 inside the dbl – see Fig. 25b. Work ½st. with this then ½st., dbl, pin at 3.

Fig. 25. Starting the leaf

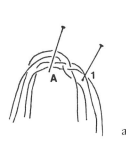

a

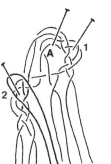

b

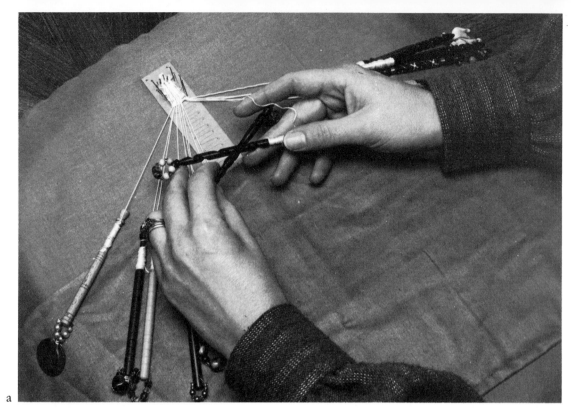

Fig. 24. Working a Bruges tie: a) tying half a reef knot b) pushing left-hand bobbin to the right (white bobbin will be tied next)

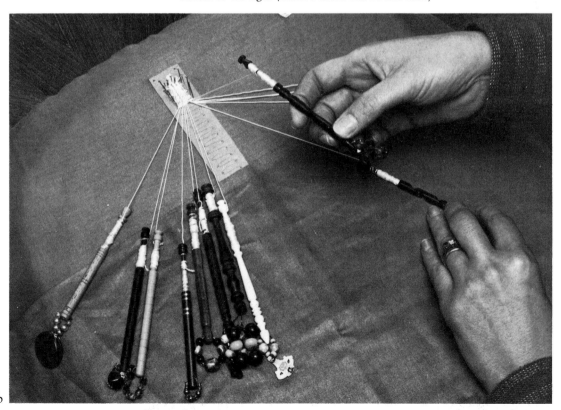

Hang 6th pr on 3 and work from right to left with dbl, 3 ½st., dbl, pin at 4.

Add final pr on 4 and work dbl, 4 ½st., dbl, pin on each row to end. Finish with a Bruges tie as above.

Mounting

Use a needle to apply a small amount of suitable adhesive, e.g. PVA or Resin W (woodwork adhesive) to the back of each piece in turn. Position and press down firmly on card or stretched fabric.

Variations

Combine several stems, leaves and flowers as a spray motif.

Redraw prickings to give longer stems, flowers of different sizes etc, choose suitable threads, e.g. sewing cotton and metallic yarn for the daisy greetings card (Fig. 26a).

Make Christmas tree decorations on the flower pricking using a glitter yarn such as Goldfingering for the wks (Fig. 26b).

Fig. 26. Variations on the flower: a) daisies b) Christmas decoration

Pricking 3. Circular mat
a) edging c) cental motif

Circular Mat (Fig. 27, Pricking 3)

Fig. 27. Circular mat

Triangles of w.st., and fans worked in dbls make up this mat which is worked in 2 pieces – an edging and a central motif.

Preparation

Make a pricking for the edging (Pricking 3a) and pin to the centre of the pillow with lettered holes on the left. Place a cover cloth across the lower half of the pricking.
Wind 9 prs (in prs) with No. 8 coton perle.

Starting

Hang 2 prs at *A* and 1 pr at each of the pins *B* to *H*.
Take the pr at *H* and go to the left by working a w.st. with each of the prs hung at *G* and *F*. Push these prs to the side while you work the fan – the wks (from *H*) will be needed at pin 9, but the 2 prs of passives (from *G* and *F*) do not come into the fan at all.

a

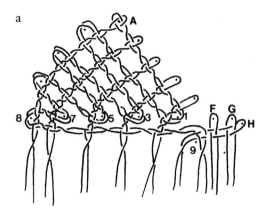

b

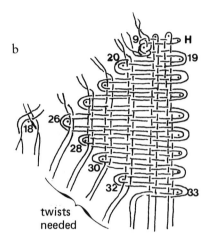

twists
needed

Fig. 28. Working details for
circular mat: a) first half of fan
b) triangle

The fan

* Work a dbl with the 2 prs at *A*, then, taking the right-hand of
these as wks, work a dbl with each of the prs hung at *B*, *C*, *D* and
E, put in a pin at *1*. Work back to the left with 5 more dbls, pin at *2*.

Work to the right again, this time with only 4 dbls – i.e. not
working the pr originally hung at *E*, pin at *3*. Four dbls to the left,
pin at *4*. Three dbls (to the right), pin at *5*. Three dbls, pin at *6*. Two
dbls, pin at *7*. Two dbls, pin at *8*.

Next work towards the centre with 6 dbls – i.e. a dbl with each
of the prs now hanging from pins *8*, *7*, *5*, *3* and *1*, plus a dbl with
the wks for the triangle (originally hung at *H*), pin at *9* (Fig. 28a).

Half of the fan is now complete – the 2nd half is the reverse of
the 1st: 6 dbls, pin at *10*. Two dbls, pin at *11*. Two dbls, pin at *12*.
Three dbls, pin at *13*. Three dbls, pin at *14*. Four dbls, pin at *15*.
Four dbls, pin at *16*. Five dbls, pin at *17*. Five dbls, pin at *18*. The 2
prs now hanging at *18* are not needed for the triangle so can be
pushed to the side.

The triangle

Take the pr now hanging at pin *9* and work to the right with 2
w.st., pin at *19*. Go to the left with 3 w.st. – i.e. bringing in 1 pr
from *17*, pin at *20*; then back to *21* with 3 w.st.

Continue working from side to side bringing in an extra pr at
each of the left-hand pins as the triangle gets wider, and leaving
out a pr as it narrows – i.e. the next row is: 4 w.st., (bringing in pair
from *15*), pin at *22*. Then: 4 w.st., pin at *23*. Four w.st. pin at *24*.
Five w.st., pin at *25*. Six w.st., pin at *26*. Six w.st., pin at *27*. Five w.
st., pin at *28* (leaving 1 pr hanging at *26*). Five w.st., pin at *29* . . .

until 3 w.st., pin at *33*, 2 w.st. The triangle is now complete.

Put the 3 right-hand prs to the side. Tw. (once) the prs hanging at *26*, *28*, *30* and *32* – this is necessary since w.st. leaves prs untwisted and you want them twisted for the dbls that follow (Fig. 28b).

Repeat from * starting with the 2 prs at *18*.

Keep turning the pillow, and moving the cover cloth so the work is always coming towards you. You can start taking out pins once you have worked 3 or 4 complete repeats of the pattern, but leave all the pins of the 1st fan and triangle in place, and also one or two pins on each side of each repeat, push these pins right down to the pricking.

Finishing

As you work the final triangle remove the starting pins so the holes can be used again. When the wks reach *H* the circle is complete.

Join the start to the finish as described for the flower head (Fig. 22), but omitting the knot (i.e. not stage 5) – it is often easier to see where you are going if you start in the centre (e.g. at pin *C*) rather than the edge of the lace.

Cut the threads approximately 15cm (6in.) from the work and remove the lace from the pillow. The next stage does require care, patience and a good light to give a neat finish, but is necessary for any item that will be washed or seen from either side. Using an appropriate sewing needle, darn each end in turn into the lace, taking one thread of each pr into the start and one into the finish and following the line of a thread as closely as possible for a few stitches. When all the ends have been darned in, flatten and shape the lace with your fingers, then trim the ends close to the work.

Next work the inner motif from Pricking 3b. This is worked in the same way as the edging except that at *O* the wks are twisted 4 times, taken round a pin at *P* and twisted 4 times again, before going back into the work. When the wks reach *P* for the 6th time

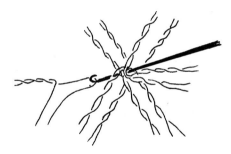

Fig. 29. Sewing through five loops

remove the pin, put a crochet hook through all 5 loops (Fig. 29); pull 1 wk through and make a sewing as described for the flower head (Fig. 22); tw. wks 4 times. Passives in the triangle will need frequent firm pulls to keep the work flat. Finish as for edging then stitch outer loops of motif to inside of edging.

Variations

1. Work just the edging and mount on a circle of fabric.
2. Work the motif on its own – e.g. for a paperweight.
3. Have a contrasting colour as wks for either the fans (hang at *A*), or the triangles (hang at *H*).
4. Use Pricking 4 and sewing cotton (Sylko 40) for a pincushion or lavender bag edging (see Fig. 11). Either start and finish as for mat edging, or start with prs hung along the centre of a fan (pins *1, 3, 5, 7, 8* and 2 prs at *9*). Begin, from *9*, with the 2nd half of a fan (i.e. 6 dbls pin at *10*), finish with a knotted join as for the flower head and cover the knots with a loop of ribbon.

Pricking 4. Pin cushion edging

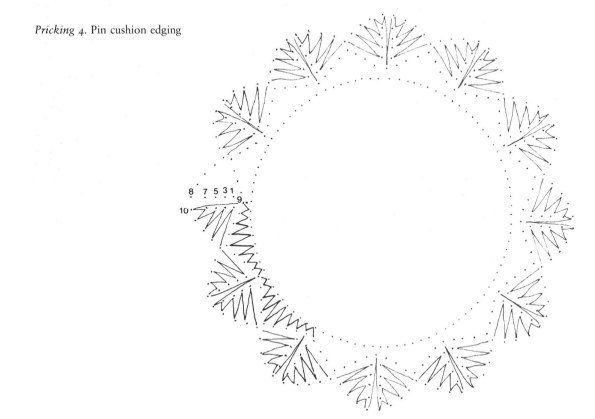

3
Torchon Lace

There are many varieties of lace. In the past lacemakers would specialise in making a type of lace peculiar to the country or area in which they lived – Maltese, Russian, Brussels, Bedfordshire, Bucks, Honiton, etc. *Torchon*, however, is a relatively simple lace which was made in many places.

Many of the typical torchon features are illustrated in the edging in Fig. 30:

a) regular geometric ground;

Fig. 30. Typical torchon edging with key to torchon edging

b) fan-shaped scallop;

c) ½st. trail;

d) spider;

e) w.st. diamond;

f) tally.

(A pricking for this edging is given in Pricking 26.)

Pricking 5. Torchon grounds

Fig. 31. Sampler of torchon grounds

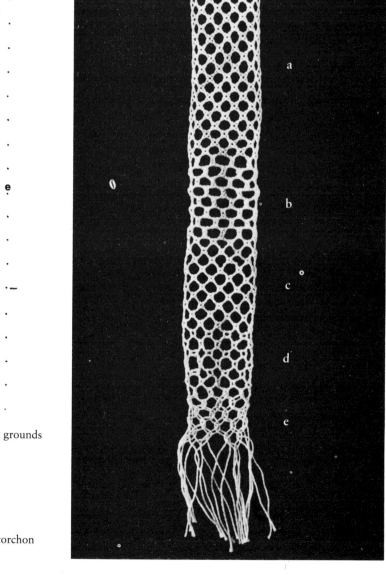

Torchon Prickings

All torchon patterns are based on a regular arrangement of pinholes and can be easily drafted on squared paper. Pricking 5 was drawn up on 6¼mm (¼in.) squares with pinholes in the centre and corners of each square – this scale is suitable for use with No. 8 coton perle (or No. 20 crochet cotton), larger or smaller squares can be used for different thicknesses of thread.

Sampler of Torchon Grounds (Fig. 31)

'Grounds' are the background stitches that show up the more solid parts of a pattern. Torchon grounds are usually worked along diagonal lines of pins.

Preparation

Make a pricking from Pricking 5. Pin with lettered holes at the top of the pillow. Wind 10 prs of bobbins with No. 8 coton perle, hang 2 prs at each of the starting pins A–E and work a dbl at each pin (or knot threads in groups of 4 and pin through the knot).

Half stitch ground (Fig. 31a)

Starting on the left take the 2nd pr from A and the 1st pr from B to work a ½st., put in a pin at 1 and work a 2nd ½st. with the same 2 prs. Take the left-hand of these prs to work a ½st. with the other pr from A, put in a pin at 2 and work another ½st. (Fig. 32a).

Next work: ½st., pin at 3, ½st. using the free pr from B and one from C. Continue working ½st., pin, ½st., following the order of pins given – pin 4 will be worked with prs from 1 and 3, pin 5 with prs from 1 and 4, and so on. Stop as the pins reach holes a–e.

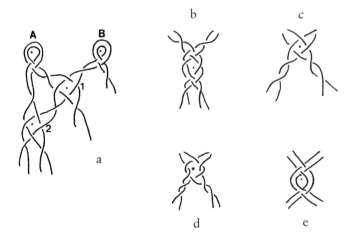

Fig. 32. Torchon ground stitches: a) ½st., pin, ½st. b) dbl, pin, dbl c) ½st., pin, ½st., tw. d) ½st., tw., pin, ½st., tw. e) w.st., pin, w.st.

Doubles ground (Fig. 31b)
Work in the order given for $\frac{1}{2}$st. ground, but work a dbl before and after every pin – start with a pr from *a* and one from *b* to work dbl, pin at *x*, dbl (Fig. 32b). The next dbl, pin, dbl is worked at *y* with a pair from *a* and one from *x* . . .

Other grounds
Stop on the next solid line and try out some other combinations of stitches, working each along the diagonal lines as before, for example:
$\frac{1}{2}$st., pin, $\frac{1}{2}$st., tw. (Figs. 31c and 32c);
$\frac{1}{2}$st., tw., pin, $\frac{1}{2}$st., tw. (Figs. 31d and 32d);
w.st., pin, w.st. (Figs. 31e and 32e).

Variations
Try these grounds in 2 or more colours – mount on petersham or ribbon for a belt or hairband.
  Work in mohair or wool on a larger grid ($12\frac{1}{2}$mm ($\frac{1}{2}$in.) squares) for a scarf or stole – strips can be linked by 'sewings'.

Flower Brooch (Fig. 33, Pricking 6)

This is made from a lace strip, consisting of fans and triangles of dbl, pin, dbl ground, worked on Pricking 6a with 9 prs.
  Fils à Dentelles is the ideal thread – it is slightly thicker and firmer than sewing cotton.

Preparation
Choose 2 toning or contrasting colours and wind 2 prs with the darker thread – one of these prs will be the wks for the fans so needs a lot of yarn, the others will be passives running along one edge. Hang wks at A, passives at H. Wind 7 prs with the lighter thread, hang these at pins B to G, with 2 prs at G. (See Pricking 6c.)

Fan
* Work in dbls exactly as in the circular edging (Fig. 27) – for the 1st row of 5 dbls use the prs from B to F with the wks from A. Bring in 1 pr from G to work the pin 9.

Triangle
After pin *18* leave the fan while you work the triangle of torchon ground. The passive pr hung at H will provide the gathering

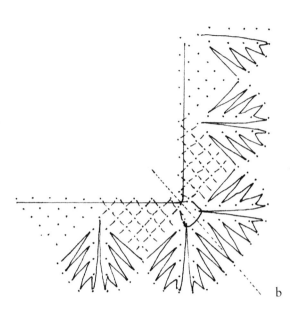

Pricking 6. a) Flower brooch
b) corner c) numbering of pin
holes

a

b

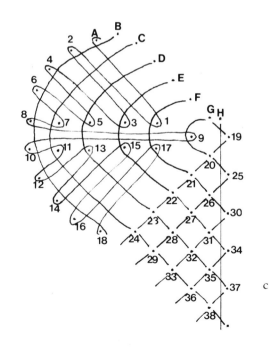

c

Fig. 33. Flower brooch: a) lace before gathering b) gathered lace with stamens and felt leaves c) completed brooch

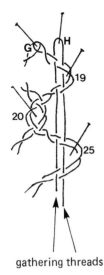

gathering threads

Fig. 34. Edge of lace strip showing gathering threads

threads so must remain untwisted throughout, therefore at *19* and all other pins on the right-hand edge (*25*, *30*, etc): work a w.st. with the passives and the pr to their left (for *19* these will be the unused pr from *G*), pin, tw. pr now on the right, w.st., tw. pr on left, Fig. 34.

Work dbl, pin, dbl at pin *20*, then at pins *21* to *24*; w.st., pin at *25* tw. right hand pr, w.st., tw. left hand pr dbl, pin, dbl at *26*, *27* . . . until pin *38* is in place.

Repeat from * to end, using prs from *18* for the start of the second fan.

Finishing

Put the passive (gathering) threads to one side. Knot the remaining threads firmly and cut close. Remove the lace from the pricking. Carefully draw up the gathering threads so the first fan comes in the centre of the flower and last on the outside, slip a small bunch of stamens in the centre and stitch in place (using one

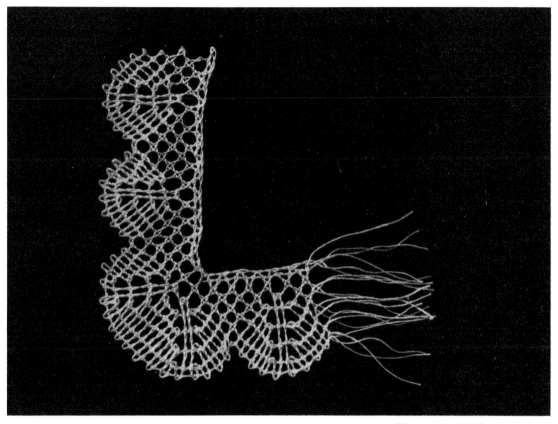

Fig. 35. Corner of an edging
worked on Pricking 6b

of the gathering threads). Cut 2 felt leaves, arrange the flower on
these and stitch. Finally stitch a safety pin or brooch clip firmly to
the back of the leaves.

Variations

1. Make a free standing flower by binding it to florists' wire.
2. Mount several flowers as a spray.
3. Use a different ground for the triangle.
4. Work leaves in w.st. or $\frac{1}{2}$st. instead of using felt.
5. Work in brown or gold as a lion's mane – use felt or card for a
face.
6. Use the same pricking, plus the corner pricking 6b, if required
to work an edging. For this an extra pr will be needed so a standard
footside can be worked – see half stitch fan edging, fig. 42, for
working of footside and corner. Fig. 35 shows the edging
worked in Bockens linen No. 50. with a ground of $\frac{1}{2}$st.,
pin, $\frac{1}{2}$st.

Fig. 36. Torchon bookmark

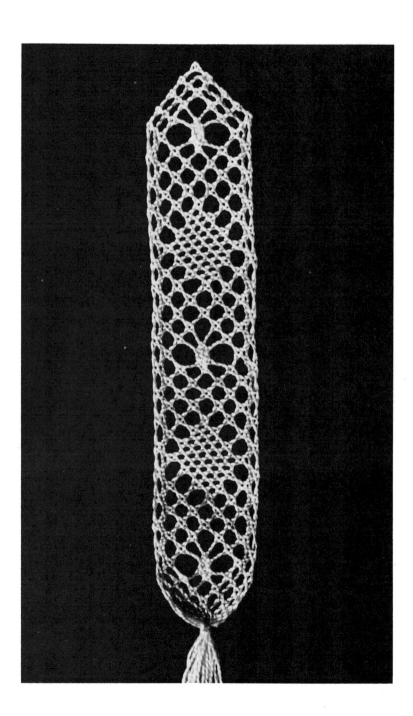

Torchon Bookmark (Fig. 36, Pricking 7)

This piece combines torchon ground ($\frac{1}{2}$st., pin, $\frac{1}{2}$st.) with spiders and $\frac{1}{2}$st. diamonds.

Pricking 7. Torchon bookmark

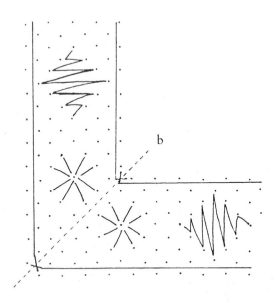

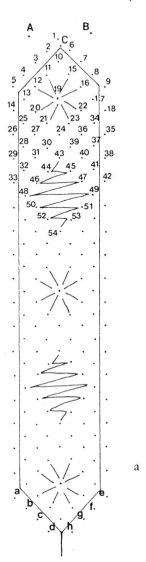

b

a

Preparation

Make a pricking from 7a including pins *A* and *B* which are *support pins*, used temporarily at the start of the piece. Wind 12 prs (in prs) with No. 8 coton perle – 10 prs in one colour, 2 prs in a contrasting colour.

Starting

Using the main colour hang 1 pr on *A* and 1 on *B*. With these work $\frac{1}{2}$st., pin at *1*, $\frac{1}{2}$st., remove loops from *A* and *B* and pull in place round *1*. * Hang another pr on *A*, work $\frac{1}{2}$st., pin at *2*, $\frac{1}{2}$st. with this and left-hand pr from *1*, remove loop from *A* and pull in place (Fig. 37a). Repeat from * for pins *3*, *4* and *5*.

Hang prs at *B* to work pins *6–9* in the same way, using right-hand pr from *1*.

Hang the 2 contrast prs across a pin at *C*, these will be passives. Take the 2 contrast bobbins on the left and work dbls with these and the 1st 4 main colour prs on that side (Fig. 37b). Use the other pr of contrasts to work 4 dbls on the right.

Working

Work $\frac{1}{2}$st., pin, $\frac{1}{2}$st. at pins *10–13*, starting with the 2 middle prs (i.e. those from *2* and *6*). Next work the edge pin: take the left-hand pr from *13* to work a dbl with the passives (contrasts)

Fig. 37. Starting the bookmark: a) using support pin – 3rd pair just released from A b) bringing in passives – contrast worked through first two pairs

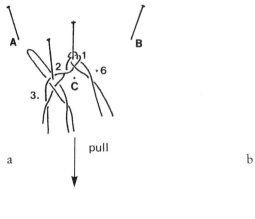

Fig. 38. Working details for bookmark: a) edge b) spider c) start of diamond

a

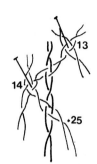

b

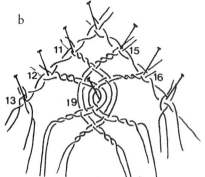

c

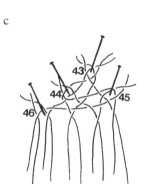

followed by ½st., pin at *14*, ½st., then work a dbl with the right-hand pr now at *14* and the passives (Fig. 38a). Leave these prs to the side and work pins *15–18* to match. NB Each time you come to the contrasts (passives) you will work a dbl with no pin.

‡ Next work a *spider* (Fig. 38b).

Twist each 'leg' (i.e. the prs at *11*, *12*, *15* and *16*) twice more.

Take a pr from *15* to work a w.st. with prs from *11* and *12*.

Take a pr from *16* to work a w.st. with prs from *11* and *12*.

Put in a pin at *19* with 2 prs on each side. Pull on bobbins to neaten top half of 'body'.

Take each pr from the right back to the left by working 2 w.st., starting as before with the 2 middle prs.

Tw. each pr 3 times. Finish off the spider with ½st., pin, ½st. at pins *20–24*.

Now work the 2 triangles of ground (*25–33* and *34–42*) with ½st., pin, ½st. at each pin and the passives worked in dbls: start with the pr that has come through the passives from *14* plus the pr from

20 to work pin 25; then dbl with the left-hand of these prs and the passives before ½st., pin at 26, ½st. then dbl with the passives again . . .

When both triangles are complete start the *half stitch diamond:* work ½st., pin, ½st. at 43, then at 44 (so far this is the same as for the ground); take the right-hand of the prs at 44 to work 2 more ½st., 1 with a pr from 43 the other with a pr from 40, pin at 45. Work back to 46 with 4 ½st. (Fig. 38c).

Continue to work from side to side, bringing in a pr at each pin and working one more ½st. on each row until pin 49 is in place. After this, work 1 less ½st. on each row so a pr is left hanging at each of pins 48–54 (6 ½st. from 49–50, 5 from 50–51 . . .), this should leave 2 prs to work the final ½st., pin, ½st. at 54.

Work 2 more triangles of ground, then repeat from ‡ until the 4th spider is complete. NB Ground stitches go right to the edge of the spider, but not to the edge of a diamond (those pinholes are needed for the working of the diamond).

Finishing

On each side bring contrasts (passives) to the centre by working 4 dbls, then work a dbl with the 2 prs of passives.

Work a final row of ½st., pin, ½st. at *a–h*. Then: work pair from *a* to the centre with 3 w.st. (i.e. with prs from *b, c* and *d*); work pr from *b* to the centre with 2 w.st.; work pr from *c* to the centre with 1 w.st. (see Fig. 39).

Work the 3 right-hand prs to the centre in the same way.

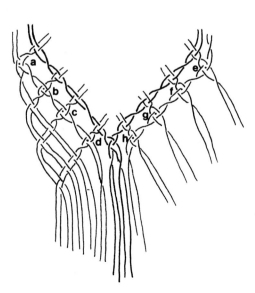

Fig. 39. Finish of bookmark

Tie the 2 outermost threads firmly round the rest.

Neaten the tassel by pulling on the bobbins, trim a few centimetres from the knot – if the knotted threads stick out darn them into the knot.

Variations

1. Work w.st. instead of $\frac{1}{2}$st. in the diamonds – prs need to be twisted after a w.st. diamond.

2. Replace spiders with diamonds – or vice versa.

3. Extend the pricking (see stage b of making a pricking in chapter 2) omitting pinholes *1–9* and *a–h*. Use the pricking to work a strip of lace, e.g. as an insertion round a skirt or across a cushion, or with the corner pricking 7b for a square of insertion (Fig. 40).

If the two ends of the lace will be joined then start on pins *10–18* (hanging on passives after pins *13* and *17*). Finish as described for circular edging.

If a straight edge is needed (e.g. when the end will be enclosed in a seam) then start and finish on a horizontal row of pins, for example *26, 27, 24, 36* and *35*, with 2 prs hung at each pin and the passives hung between *26* and *27*, and *36* and *35*.

Fig. 40. Corner of insertion worked on 7b

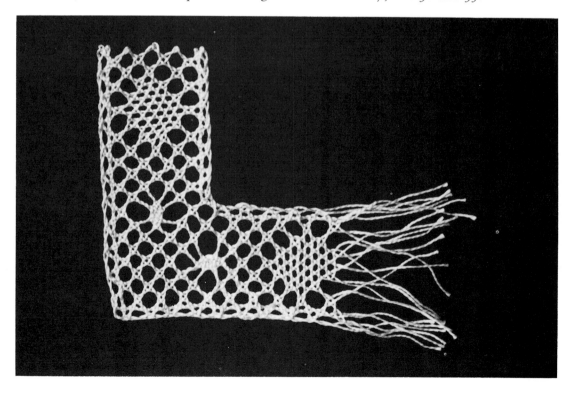

headside

Fig. 41. Edgings and insertion showing footside and headside

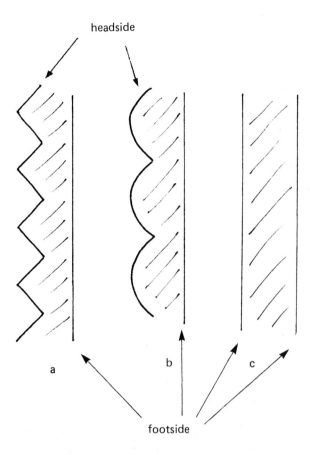

a

b

c

footside

Footside and Headside (Fig. 41)

On a length of lace edging there is usually one straight edge and one toothed (Fig. 41a) or scalloped edge (Fig. 41b). The (straight) edge which is sewn onto the fabric is called the footside, while the free (scalloped) edge is the headside.

Footsides can be curved, e.g. circular edging Fig. 27.

Lace intended as an insertion has two footsides (Fig. 41c).

English lacemakers have traditionally worked with the headside on the left, while most continental lace is made with the headside on the right.

The form of footside that is most common in torchon lace – the *standard footside* – is the one produced on the bookmark above. The method of working is however slightly different in that instead of the $\frac{1}{2}$st., pin, $\frac{1}{2}$st. on the edge, a dbl is worked and the pin put beside the dbl – see *half stitch fan edging* on page 47.

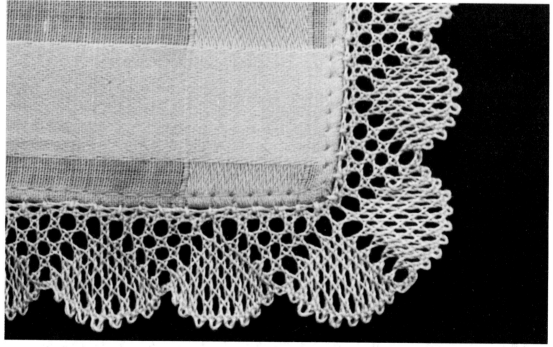

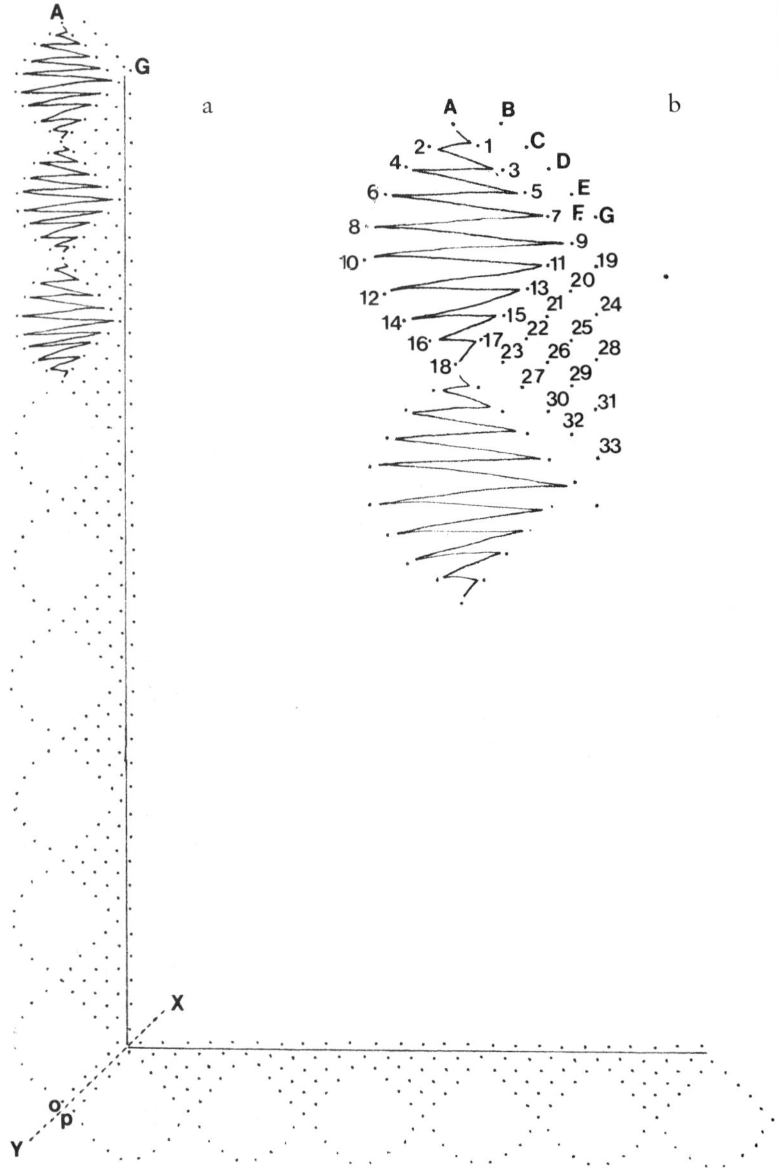

a

b

A   B

A   B   .C

2.   .1   .D

4.   .3   .E

6.   .5   .E

8.   .7   F .G

.9

10.   .11   .19

.13   20

12.   21   .24

14.   .15 22   25

16.   .17 23   26   .28

18.   27   29

30   .31

32

.33

X

O
P

Y

Half Stitch Fan Edging (Fig. 42)

When you work the next piece you will be adding a little more lace to the many hundreds of miles that have been worked from this pattern over the past two or three centuries. It is one of the simplest of the traditional patterns so could be made both by the young girls (and boys) who were just learning the lacemaking trade, and by the old when they could no longer work the more

Fig. 42. *opposite*
a) Handkerchief with half stitch fan edging b) close-up of handkerchief edging

complicated designs. Most of the lace was worked in very long lengths and sold by the yard so needed to be folded or gathered when trimming anything with a corner. A worked corner, as given here (Fig. 42b), produces a neater and more satisfying result.

Handkerchief edging

You will need: a small handkerchief; a reel of sewing cotton (e.g. Sylko 40) in chosen colour and 9 prs of bobbins.

Using Pricking 8a, mark the diagonal corner line (X–Y) in red, pin to the pillow with A–G to the left of top centre. This pricking will allow a small edging (up to 20cm (8in.) from corner to corner) to be worked without moving the lace too often, for a longer edging extend the pricking before or after the corner.

Wind bobbins in prs. Hang 2 prs at A, 1 pr at each of B–F and 2 prs at G. (The pr at F will be passives.) See Pricking 8b.

Take the right-hand pr to work a dbl with the other pr at G and one with the pr at F, leave these prs to the side.

Work a dbl with the 2 prs at A.

The fan

* Take the 2nd pr from the left to work ½st., pin at *1* with the pr from B (Fig. 43a). Work back towards the left with ½st., dbl, pin at *2*. Remove pin B and pull the bobbin to eliminate the loop (Fig. 43b).

Next row: dbl, 2 ½st., pin at *3* (this brings in pr from C) (Fig. 43c). Then: 2 ½st., dbl, pin at *4*. Remove pin C.

Continue the fan bringing in the pr from D at *5*, the pr from E at *7* and the pr that has come across from G at *9*. As the fan gets wider each pair of rows will have one more ½st. than the last. Remove pins D and E and eliminate loops.

After pin *9* the fan gets narrower: while continuing to work dbls before and after the pin on the left-hand edge, work one ½st.

Fig. 43. Starting the half stitch fan

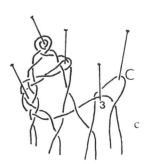

a

b

c

less on the right of the fan so two threads are left out at each of pins *9, 11, 13, 15* and *17* (as in ½st. diamond of the bookmark) – the row after pin *9* will be: 5 ½st., dbl, pin at *10*, the next row: dbl, 4 ½st., pin at *11* . . .

The triangle

You should finish the fan with 2 prs to work dbl, pin at *18*, dbl. Leave these on the left and work the first of the *footside* pins with the 3 right-hand prs: take pr from *9* and work to the right with two dbls (i.e. with passives, from *F*, and the edge pr); put in a pin at *19* between the 2 dbls (Fig. 44a); enclose the pin by working a dbl with the passives and the 2nd pr from the right (Fig. 44b).

To summarise the standard footside: it is worked with 3 prs, 3 dbls and 1 pin.

a 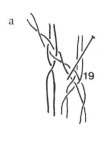 b 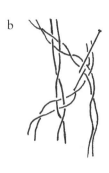 c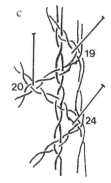

Fig. 44. Standard footside: a) pin placed beside second double b) three doubles worked c) second footside pin worked

Work a line of ½st., pin, ½st., ground at *20–23*, working pin *20* with the left-hand pr of the 3 that worked the footside plus the pr from *11*.

Complete the triangle (to pin *33*) working footside pins on the edge (pins *24, 28*, etc) and ½st., pin, ½st. at remaining pins.

Work the 2nd fan as the 1st from *, working the 1st ½st. with 1 pr from *18* and 1 from *23*.

Work alternate fans and triangles until you have reached, but not crossed, the (red) corner line, finishing with dbl, pin at *o*, dbl.

The corner

Quarter turn the pillow so that the start of the lace is on your right. Work a dbl with the 2 right-hand prs (this will result in a different pr becoming the passives) and leave to the side.

Put in a pin at *p* between the 2 prs from *o*, dbl with these prs. Repeat from *. (The directions of the prs across the corner are indicated on Pricking 9 – a larger version of Pricking 8.)

Continue to the end of the pricking. Before moving the lace work out how many pattern repeats you need for each side. Always make your lace a little longer than the piece on which it is to be mounted – lace contracts slightly when the pins are removed and may shrink a little when washed. Calculate the number of repeats required by dividing the length of the edge by the length of one pattern repeat. For example if you are using a 20cm (8in.) handkerchief and this edging, in which one repeat is 1.6cm ($\frac{5}{8}$in.), the sum is $20 \div 1.6 = 12.5$ (8in. $\div \frac{5}{8}$in. $= 12\frac{1}{2}$in. approximately). The number of complete repeats required is therefore 13. An extra half fan is needed on each end for the corners so each side will have 13 triangles of ground and 14 fans. (NB Bought handkerchiefs are not always completely square – base your calculations on the longest side.)

Once you have decided on the number of repeats move the lace (as described on page 21) to the appropriate place at the start of the pricking (having first moved the pricking slightly) and repin at least 1 complete repeat, also put in a pin where the passives go round the corner. Check that your hanky will fit comfortably between the worked corner and the corner of the pricking (Fig. 45a).

Continue with the lace until all 4 corners have been worked and there is enough on the last length to match up with the start (Fig. 45b).

Fig. 45. Working a square of edging: a) first move b) final section

Finishing

Pin the start of the lace (at least one repeat) to the pricking immediately below the last worked row of pins. Check that the

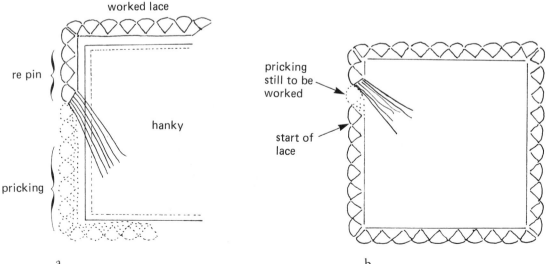

worked lace

re pin

pricking

hanky

a

pricking still to be worked

start of lace

b

lace is not twisted and that opposite sides have the same number of repeats.

Join the start to the finish as described for the circular edging. Do not remove pins from the last 2 or 3 repeats until sewings are complete or you will distort the lace – push the pins down to allow room to work. *Mount* the lace with the same thread used for working: start with 2 tiny stitches in the fabric then bring the needle out of the fold of the hem; * through the footside pinhole; back into the same point on the hem; inside the hem to below the next pinhole; repeat from * (Fig. 46). As you work, ease (gather) the lace to take up any fullness. Fasten off firmly. Press the completed handkerchief under a damp cloth.

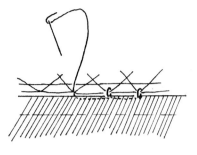

Fig. 46. Mounting an edging

Variations (Fig. 47, Prickings 9 and 10)

1. For a mat or tray-cloth edging use Pricking 9 with No. 8 coton perle (or No. 40 crochet cotton, No. 35 linen etc.)
2. Work w.st. or dbls instead of $\frac{1}{2}$st. on the fans – with or without a contrast pr as the wks. See spider and fan edging (Fig. 66).
3. Replace $\frac{1}{2}$st. in the ground with dbls, or work spiders (Fig. 38b)

Fig. 47. Variations on the half stitch fan edging
a) *top centre* Sampler of fans and triangles: *Fans:* 1) w.st., 2) w.st. with dbls on edge separated by 1–3 twists, 3) w.st., dbls on edge, passives twisted at widest point, 4) dbls, w.st. for middle four rows; *Triangles:* 1) dbl pin dbl ground, 2) spider in $\frac{1}{2}$st. ground, 3) one tally in $\frac{1}{2}$st. ground, 4) two tallies in $\frac{1}{2}$st. ground
b) child's collar

Pricking 9. Larger scale version of Pricking 8

or tallies (Fig. 67) within the triangles (Fig. 47a).

4. Work on a curve for a collar (Fig. 47b) – Pricking 10. This has a slightly deeper fan so needs 10 prs (No. 20 crochet cotton). The collar is started and finished with a corner which allows the threads at the end to be hidden in the neck of the garment. Start with 1 pr on *A*, 2 prs on each of *B*, *C* and *D*, 3 prs on *E*. Work right-hand pr across to pin *1* in dbls. Work back to the right with dbl, 5 $\frac{1}{2}$st., pin at 2 (this leaves 3 prs on the right for the footside) then complete the fan in the normal way. Turn the pillow after pin *11* and work along the pricking. Move work when required and transfer to Pricking 10b for the finish, again turning the pillow when you reach the corner line. Finish with a Bruges tie.

5. Use Pricking 10 without the corner sections for a circular edging.

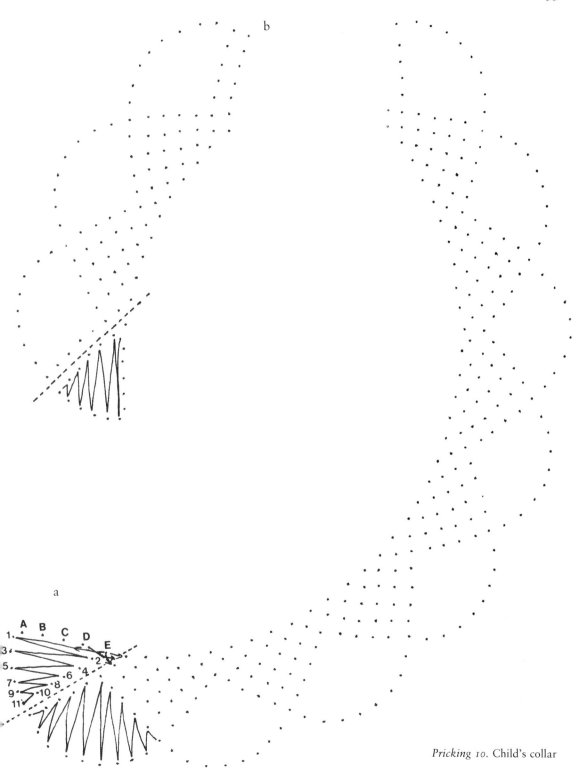

b

a

A B C D E
1.
3.
5.
7.
9. 10
11

Pricking 10. Child's collar

4
Braids and Braid Lace

Several types of lace are based on relatively narrow braids (tapes). For some of this lace a straight bobbin-made or woven braid is gathered or folded and sewn in shape, the spaces are then filled with needlepoint (buttonhole) stitches. Other laces are worked entirely on the pillow with the braid shaped and joined to itself as the work progresses. Much lace of this type has been made in Russia and other eastern European countries, hence its common name of 'Russian tape lace'.

Braids are simple to work, requiring relatively few bobbins – they can be straight, curved, looped or shaped into motifs, mats or edgings, and made in colours and textures to suit any need.

Straight Braids

The simplest braid is probably the w.st. sample (Fig. 9a) worked on Pricking 1 (chapter 2). Many other braids can be worked on this pricking, or a larger or smaller version of it. With braid lace, unlike torchon, there is no fixed number of prs for each pattern – if you are using a thick yarn then you use few prs, but if your work looks thin and flimsy then use more passive prs, or put in extra tws for firmness. Figure 48 gives some examples.

Fig. 48a – Ladder braid worked on Pricking 1 using 5 prs No. 8 or 5 coton perle or No. 20 crochet cotton. Wks hung at A and 2 prs passives at each of B and D. Each row: 2 w.st., tw. wks 3 times, 2 w.st., tw. wks, pin. Thread narrow ribbon through finished braid for a bookmark, Christmas bauble, trim for a baby's dress, etc.

Fig. 48b and c – Narrow braids worked on Pricking 11: b) 2 prs wool as passives, one pr sewing cotton as wks – w.st. with wks twisted at pins: c) 5 prs (2 prs Gutterman metallic as edge prs + 3 prs sewing cotton) – dbl, $2\frac{1}{2}$st., dbl, pin on each row – this will

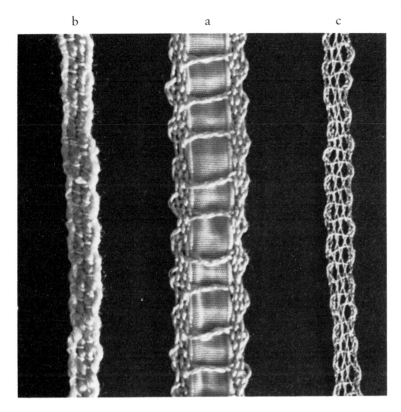

Fig. 48. Simple braids: a) ladder braid b) whole stitch braid c) half stitch braid with doubles on the edge

Pricking 11. Narrow braids

probably twist when removed from the pillow, it can be fixed flat or to show off the twist.

Cable and chain (Fig. 49)
These feature contrast threads as raised lines or dots. Try samples on Pricking 1 with a glitter yarn (e.g. 'Goldfingering'), or DK wool as the contrasts on a crochet cotton background.

Chain (Fig. 49a)
Wind 1 pr with gold and 1 pr with silver, link these 2 prs and hang on C (without the link the chain could unravel), placing the silver threads between the gold.

Wind 7 prs with crochet cotton No. 20: hang 2 prs at A, 2 prs at B and 3 prs at D.

Taking the left-hand pr as wks: dbl with the other pr from A, 2 w.st. (with prs from B), go through 2 contrast prs as a chain, i.e

Fig. 49. a) Chain b) cable
c) cable worked with one
contrast thread d) chain
worked with two contrast
threads

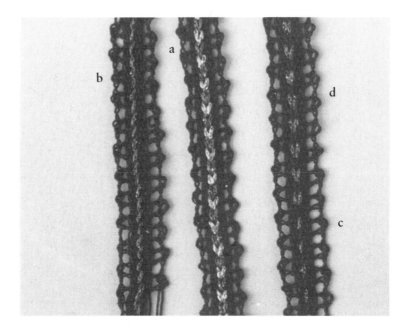

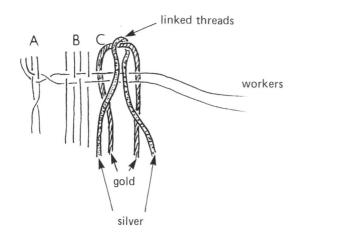

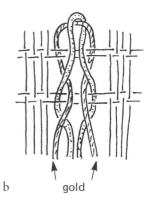

Fig. 50. Working a chain:
a) first row b) second row

lift 2 inside (silver) threads; pass wks underneath; replace bobbins on the pillow so silver threads are outside the gold (Fig. 50a) work 2 more w.st., tw. wks, dbl, pin.

The 2nd row is like the 1st, i.e. dbl, 2 w.st., chain, 2 w.st., tw. wks, dbl, pin – on this row it will be the gold threads that are lifted, then put down outside the silver once the wks have passed through (Fig. 50b).

Repeat the 2 rows as required.

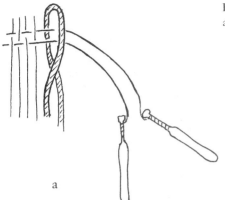

Fig. 51. Working a cable:
a) first row b) second row

Cable (Fig. 49b)

This uses just 1 pr of contrasts. If carrying on from the chain sample turn back the silver threads and continue with the gold (or vice versa), alternatively start again with just 1 contrast pr at C.

While working the rest of the braid as before, each time you reach the contrasts pick up the one on the right, pass the wks underneath and put the contrast down to the left of its pr – this has the effect of twisting the contrasts between the rows (Fig. 51).

Variations

For spots of colour work a cable with 1 thread of main colour and 1 thread of contrast (Fig. 49c).
For V-shaped spots work a chain with 2 contrasts alternating with 2 main colour threads (Fig. 49d).

Shaping braids

Braids can be made to follow almost any line. Smooth curves and loops are easiest to work – with these it is simply a matter of positioning the pinholes on the inside of the braid closer together than those on the outside. Where a braid is angled, or sharply curved, the inside pins can be used twice or *turning stitches* worked. Where 2 parts of the braid touch they are usually linked by *sewings*.

Looped Braid (Fig. 52a, Pricking 12)

Three prs DK wool as passives and 1 pr sewing cotton as wks. Hang wks at *A*, passives at *B*, *C* and *D* – in this example the pr at *D* are contrasts.

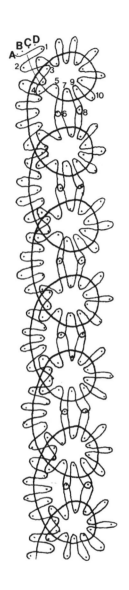

Pricking 12. Looped braid

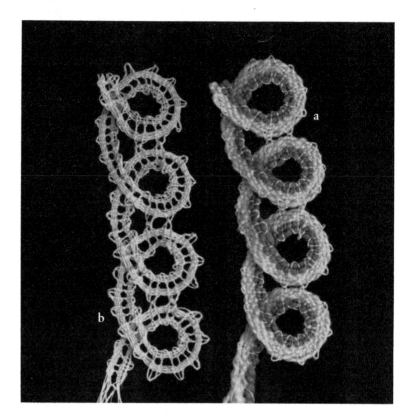

Fig. 52. Looped braids: a) wool passives, sewing cotton for workers b) Fils à Dentelles

Work 3 st., tw. wks twice, pin on every row, working pins in order and turning the pillow as required to keep the bobbins coming towards you. Remove pins 3 and 4 before working the braid across itself, push other pins well down and cover with a cloth. When the braid comes to pin 8 for the 2nd time twist the wks and make a sewing as follows: remove pin; use a crochet hook to pull a loop of 1 of the wks through the pin space; pass bobbin of other wk through loop; pull tight and tw. (see 1 to 4 of finishing p 24).

Make a 2nd sewing at 6. Complete 2nd loop of braid.

Work 3rd loop of braid with sewings to 2nd, and so on.

Variations

Try other braids on the same pricking, 52b for example is a ladder braid worked with 6 prs Fils à Dentelles (with workers twisted twice at pins and between 2nd and 3rd passives from the inside) – the first row is: 3 w.st., tw. wks twice, 2 w.st., pin, tw. wks twice.

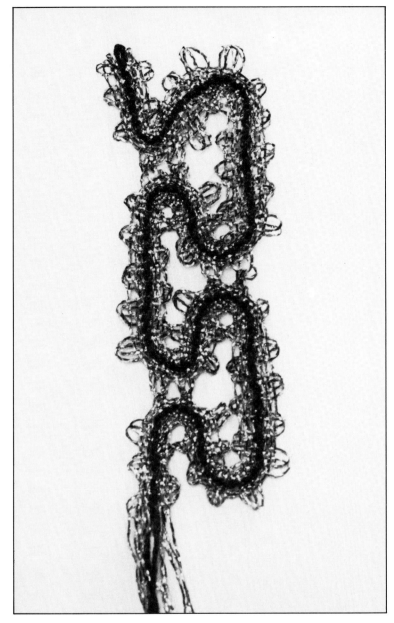

Fig. 53. Greek key braid

Greek Key Braid (Fig. 53, Pricking 13)

In this the braid changes direction sharply on each bend so turning stitches are needed (shown on the pricking by >, without a pinhole).

This example was worked in w.st. with 5 prs Gutterman metallic thread (passives and wks) and a central cable of 1 pr No. 8 coton perle. Other braids and combinations of relatively fine threads (e.g. sewing cotton) could be used.

Start the braid with wks at A, passives and cable at B and C.

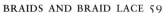
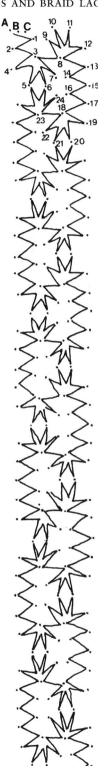

Pricking 13. Greek key braid

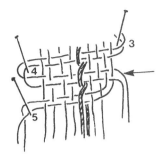

Fig. 54. Whole stitch used as a turning stitch

Work in the normal way, i.e. 2 w.st., cable, 2 w.st., tw. wks, pin on each row, until pin 4 is in place. * Work back across the braid, leave the wks and take the inside passives as wks for the next row: w.st., cable, 2 w.st., pin at 5 (Fig. 54). Repeat from * twice more – 3 turning stitches worked.

After pin 7 work across the braid and make a sewing at 3. Continue with the braid working turning stitches and sewings as required (turning stitches between 9 and 12, and 19 and 22, sewings at 8, 18 etc).

Greek key motif (Fig. 55, Pricking 14)
The general method for working this is the same as for the braid, however there are no sewings inside the loops, and only one sewing connecting inner loops. Start, and finish, at S. Finish as described for beaded disc, below.

Designing for braid lace (Fig. 56)
Several braid motifs are given below, but you could easily design your own. Initials are an obvious choice so a flowing A has been used as an example of the steps from idea to finished piece.
1. Sketch the shape (Fig. 56a). Decide where you will start and finish – note change in position of finish between Fig. 56a and

Fig. 55. Box showing Greek key braid and motif

Pricking 14. Greek key motif

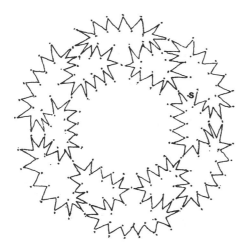

Fig. 56b to allow finish to be hidden on part of the braid.

2. Redraw outline as a continuous double line (Fig. 56b).

3. Space pinholes along outside of curves.

4. Mark pinholes and turning stitches on the inside of curves.

5. Trace complete pattern and turn over before pricking – the motif can then be worked with the wrong side uppermost (Fig. 56c).

6. Select the braid and suitable threads, remembering that where turning stitches are needed the inside passives must be the same yarn as the wks.

7. Work motif with sewings where the braid touches or crosses itself (Fig, 56d). In this example 5 prs of machine embroidery thread (black) and 1 pr Gutterman metallic (gold) were used for a w.st. braid with central cable.

Fig. 56. Braid initial: a) first sketch b) initial as a double line c) reversed pricking

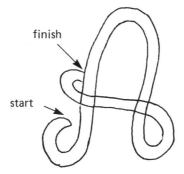

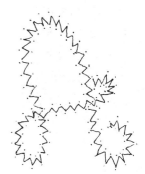

a   b   c

56d. completed initial

Fig. 57. Beaded disc

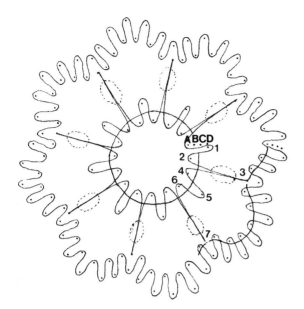

Beaded Disc (Fig. 57, Pricking 15)

Six prs. Hang 1 pr wks (sewing cotton) at *A*, 2 prs passives (No. 5 or 8 coton perle) at each of *B* and *D*, and 1 pr for the cable (wool or glitter yarn) at *C*.

Work a w.st. braid with central cable for the inner ring, making long picots at pins 3, 7, etc. – i.e. work 2 w.st., cable, 2 w.st., pin on each row, at the end of the 3rd row make a *picot* as follows: tw. wks twice, put in a pin at 3 and take just 1 of the threads round the pin from bottom to top, tw. twice again (Fig. 58). (This is the easiest way of forming a picot – there are at least 3 others.)

When the ring is complete link the 2 ends with sewings; tie off with a Bruges tie – do not tie the thick threads, just trap them between the knots; cut close.

Slip a bead onto each picot – using a crochet hook (Fig. 59a).

Work outer braid as inner, but at 3, 7, etc use the inside passives to make a sewing to the picot, Fig. 59b (this is the 'exception that proves the rule' since sewings are almost always made with the wks). Finish as for inner ring, leaving one thread for hanging.

Variations

1. Choose another type of braid.
2. Omit beads for a flat motif.

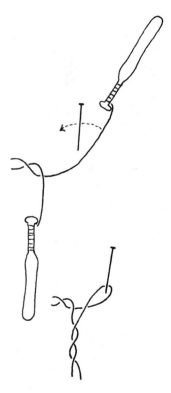

Fig. 58. Making a picot

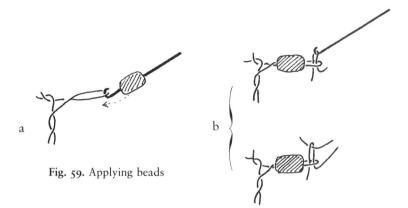

Fig. 59. Applying beads

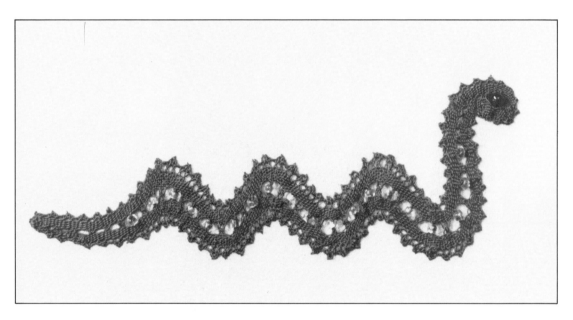

Fig. 60. Nessie

Nessie (Fig. 60, Pricking 16)

Worked in sewing cotton (6 prs) with small beads applied to picots along the mid-line.

Start at tip of tail with 5 prs (passives) on *P*, wks on *W*. Work along the back with 4 w.st. and 1 dbl on each row – the dbl is on the outside edge, remember to twist the wks when going from w.st. to dbls. In the centre line work a picot where there is to be a bead, at other pins twist wks twice. Work turning stitches where necessary.

After working the picot for the eye, work the rest of the head in w.st. Thread a black bead onto the picot and 'sew' in place.

Go along the underside, with sewings in the centre and dbls on

Pricking 16. Nessie

the outside, slipping a bead on to each picot before the sewing. Finish: discard 1 pr on each of the last 4 rows by putting the bobbins to the back of the pillow (Fig. 61). Sew final 2 prs to tip of tail and darn in these ends, cut discarded threads close.

Coaster (Fig. 62, Pricking 17)

You will need 7 prs No. 8 coton perle. Hang 2 prs at *A*, 3 prs at *B*, 2 prs at *C*.

Fig. 62. Coaster

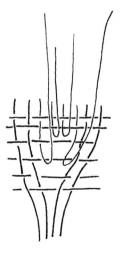

Fig. 61. Discarding pairs

* Starting on the left work 5 $\frac{1}{2}$st., dbl, pin (at *1*). Work back across the braid with dbl, 5 $\frac{1}{2}$st., pin (at *2*).

Repeat from * all round, turning the pillow, working the braid across itself and making sewings as required (see looped braid Fig. 52).

Finish: when the work reaches X–Y ease the start of the braid from under the final loop and repin (through the work) at *ABC*. Work the dbl, 5 $\frac{1}{2}$st. from Y to A then tie off as described for beaded disc.

Variations

1. Mat from 7 coasters (Fig. 63). Work 1 coaster, remove from the pricking and pin to pillow so pinholes *R, S* and *T* of 1 loop are close to the equivalent holes on the pricking: work 2nd coaster making sewings at these pins; sew 3rd, 4th, 5th and 6th coasters to 2 adjacent ones; sew 7th to 3 others to complete the ring.

Further coasters could be added, as in patchwork or crochet.

(The coasters in Fig. 63 were worked with just 6 prs giving a more open braid.)

Pricking 17. Coaster

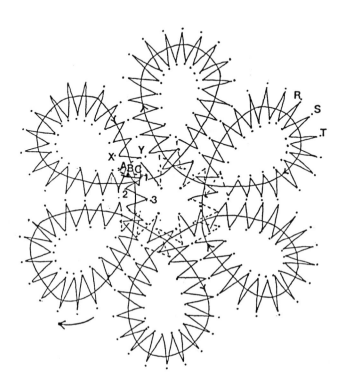

Fig. 63. Mat from seven coasters

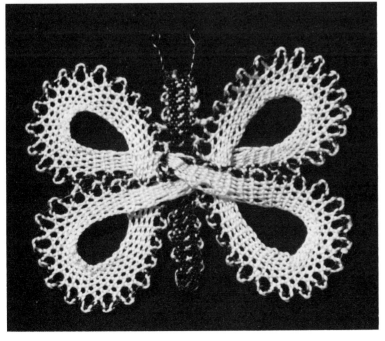

Fig. 64. Butterfly

Pricking 18. Butterfly

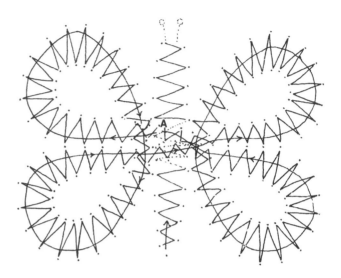

2. The butterfly in Fig. 64 uses 4 of the braid loops as wings. Start at *A* on Pricking 18, work the 2 left-hand wings then across to top right. As you cross the centre of the body start working the dbls on the left of the braid instead of the right, also take across (in w.st.) any contrast edge pr – this keeps the 2 sides symmetrical.

Work the body as for the flower stem (Fig. 23), starting at the tail and making sewings where it touches the wings. Finish with a Bruges tie – leave 2 threads uncut, thread a bead on each and darn back into work as antennae.

For a free standing butterfly, wind a flexible wire with 1 thread of the edge pr on the wings, and with the 2 outside threads of the body.

Cat (Fig. 65, Pricking 19)

Six prs Sylko – a black cat makes an ideal motif for a Good Luck card.

This is worked in the same braid as the coaster, i.e. dbl on the outside of the curve, $\frac{1}{2}$st. across the rest of the braid.

Start with 4 prs at tip of the tail (*T*); $\frac{1}{2}$st. with the 2 left-hand prs, pin at *1*. Work cross the braid with 2 $\frac{1}{2}$st., dbl, pin at *2*. Hang a pr on *2* positioning the bobbins as 3rd pr from the right (as for the leaf, Fig. 25); work across the braid with dbl, 3 $\frac{1}{2}$st., pin at *3*. Add 6th pr on pin *4* and work rest of braid with 4 $\frac{1}{2}$st. and 1 dbl on each row. Where turning stitches are needed work just a $\frac{1}{2}$st. before going back across the braid with the 2nd pr from the left.

Put 2 tw. in the prs that go round *a*, *b*, *c* and *d* – this gives a firmer loop which makes it easier to take sewings on the return.

Work picots (Fig. 58) for the whiskers.

The braid turns sharply at the ears so several turning stitches are needed – if this distorts your lace work ½st., pin, ½st. instead of some of the turning stitches, removing pin R and replacing it in the same hole as often as required.

Make sewings at *d–a*.

Finishing

Make sewings to the edge of the tail at *s–t*. After each sewing work 1 stitch then turn the pr just worked to the back of the pillow before continuing with the braid. After the final sewing, knot all the threads firmly and cut close.

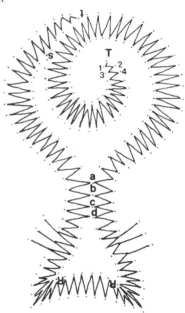

Fig. 65. Cat

Pricking 19. Cat

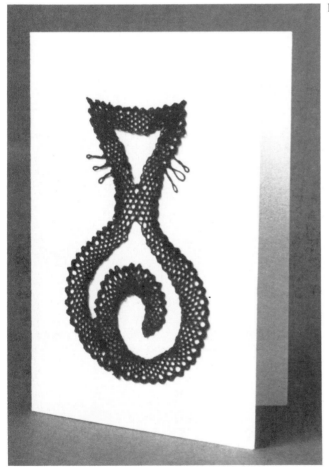

5
More Torchon

Spider and Fan Edging (Fig. 66, Pricking 20)

If you have worked the earlier torchon pieces you should have little trouble with this edging – the only new technique is the working of a square *tally* within the ground section (the tally could be omitted and ½st., pin, ½st. worked in its place).

Tallies (also known as almonds, leaves, leadworks or plaits) are the small woven blocks found in many varieties of lace. In torchon they are often square or rectangular, but can be triangular or leaf-shaped.

Fig. 66. Spider and fan edging

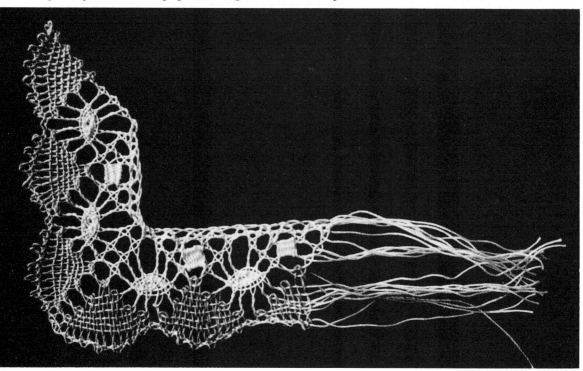

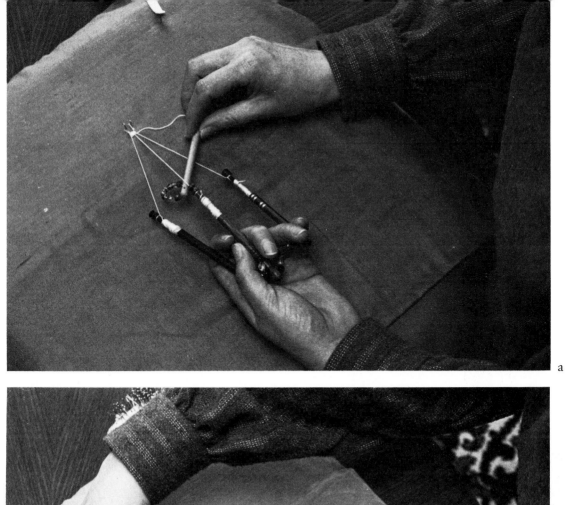

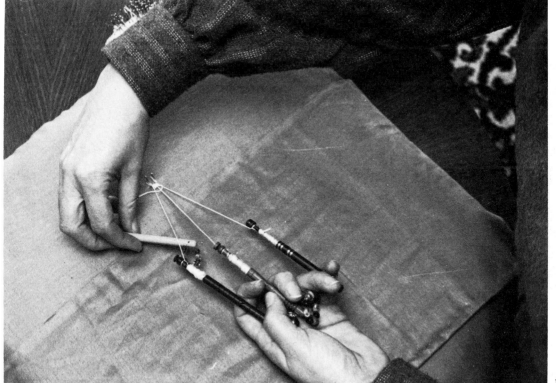

Fig. 67. Working a tally: a) start of a weaving b) return movement

Each tally is worked with 2 prs of bobbins. To practise a rectangular tally wind 4 bobbins with coton perle, knot in prs and pin, through the knots, about 5mm (¼in.) apart; tw. both prs; hold 3 bobbins between the fingers of your left hand with the 2 outer threads parallel; take the 4th bobbin in your right hand and weave it over and under the other threads (reverse if left handed) (Fig. 67). Six weavings – i.e. going from 1 side to the other and back 6 times – will give an almost square tally, use more or less weavings as required. At the end of the tally tw. both prs twice. Support the tally with a pin on each side and try a 2nd one (Fig. 68a).

NB If you pull on the weaver once the other 3 threads have been released, the tally will become distorted (Fig. 68b). To avoid this always take the pr without the weaver into the work first (the weaver can start or finish on either side). Putting the weaver to the back of the pillow until required will reduce the chance of an accidental pull.

Fig. 68. a) Square tally
b) distortion of tally following pull on the weaver

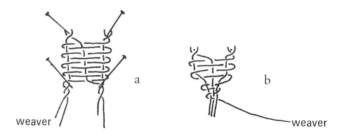

Working the edging

Use Pricking 20, extending it if required for a longer edging. Wind 11 prs with Fils à Dentelles – 10 prs 1 colour, 1 pr contrast. Start with contrasts and one other pr on *A*, remaining prs on support pins *B* (4 prs) and *C* (5 prs) to be brought in as required.

Pins *1–14* outline a w.st. fan with dbls on the outside edge, which is worked in the same way as the ½st. fan in Fig. 42. Start as follows: * taking contrasts as wks, dbl (with other pr at *A*) w.st. (with 1st pr from *B*) pin at *1*, w.st., tw. wks (this twist is necessary when going from w.st. to dbls), dbl, pin at *2*. Dbl, 2 w.st. (bringing in 2nd pr from *B*), pin at *3*. Two w.st., tw. wks, dbl, pin at *4*, and so on until the fan is complete. Remove pin *B* and eliminate the loops.

Work ½st., pin, ½st. at pins *15–17* (bringing in three of the prs from *C*) and a footside pin at *18* (bringing in the final 2 prs).

Next work a spider, centre pin *19*, with 6 prs – the method of

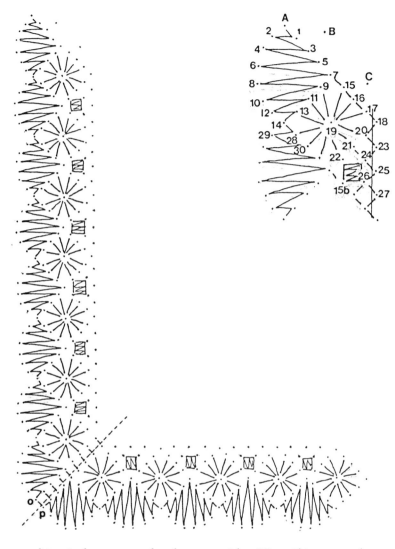

Pricking 20. Spider and fan edging

working is the same as for the 4 pr spider (Fig. 38b) except that 3 w.st. (instead of 2) are worked to take each pr from one side to the other (Fig. 69).

Pins 20–27 make up a triangle of ½st., pin, ½st. ground with a standard footside, just before working pin 26 work a tally of 6 weavings with the pr from 24 and one from 22, finish with the weaver on the left and its bobbin placed to the back of the pillow until required (at *15b*).

Repeat from *, working the corners and finishing as for the half stitch fan edging. To keep the contrasts in the right place at the corner work ½st. before pin *o* and after *p*, with a dbl between the pins.

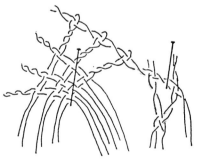

Fig. 69. First half of six-legged spider

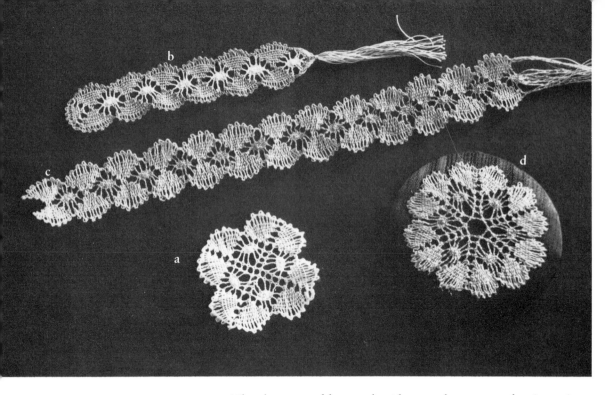

Fig. 70. Spider and fan variations: a) square b) bookmark c) decorative strip d) six-sided motif

The elements of fans and spiders can be put together in various other ways as illustrated in Fig. 70.

Square (Fig. 70a, Pricking 21)

Putting 4 corners together produces a square motif, the footside and $\frac{1}{2}$st. ground disappear and only 10 prs are needed.

Make the pricking, marking the diagonal lines (W–X, Y–Z) in red. Start with 2 prs at *A* and remaining prs temporarily on pins to the right of W–X. Work as for edging, stopping and turning the pillow at the red lines. Finish as flower head.

Bookmark (Fig. 70b, Pricking 22)

Replacing the footside and ground with a 2nd line of fans produces a decorative strip which can be adapted as a bookmark.

Start with your threads (10 prs Fils à Dentelles) laid across the pillow: 4 prs resting on a pin at 7, 2 prs on each of 8, 10 and 12 – if using 2 colours have 4 prs of 1 colour (on 7) and 6 prs of the other.

Use the 4 bobbins to the left of 7 to work dbl, pin at *A*, dbl (Fig. 71), then work as far as pin 6, bringing in the left-hand threads from 8 at 1, from 10 at 3, etc. (the 1st 3 rows will be: w.st., pin at 1; w.st., tw. wks, dbl, pin at 2; dbl, 2 w.st., pin at 3). Take wks across to 25 but do not put in a pin.

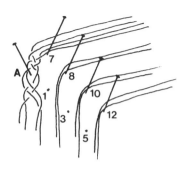

Fig. 71. Starting with threads laid across the pillow

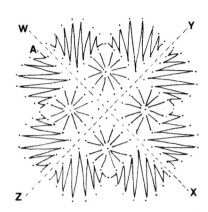

Pricking 21. Square motif

Turn pillow so the top of the pricking is on your right. Remove pin 7 and replace between the 2 prs of the dbl. Remove pins 8, *10* and *12*. Work top fan, starting with dbl, w.st., pin at 8 and continuing to dbl, pin at *17*.

Turn pillow to original position and work right-hand fan as far as pin 24, then work across with dbl, 4 w.st., pin at *25* – the 4th w.st. will bring in the wks from the left hand fan. After the pin work another w.st. with the 2 wk prs which will take them to their original sides.

* Complete both fans then work the 1st spider. Work the top halves of the next 2 fans, link the 2 wks at the centre pin and repeat from * to end. Finish as for the 1st bookmark (Fig. 39).

Pricking 22. Bookmark

Decorative strip (Fig. 70c)
This is worked in the same way and on the same pricking as the bookmark, but does not need the top fan. Start as for the edging, either with a fan and a spider or with 2 fans (*A* and *18*), hanging prs temporarily on support pins.

Variations
1. Many of the variations suggested for the half stitch fan edging (Fig. 49) can be applied to this pattern, including changing the scale for use with threads of different thickness. Fig. 72 shows a small section of the edging drafted on squared paper – in a and b

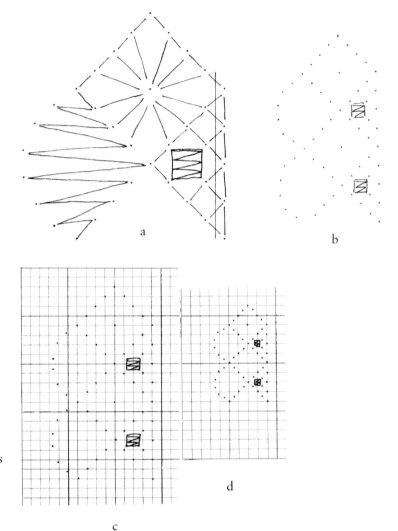

Fig. 72. Torchon pattern
drafted on squared paper:
a) using alternate 5mm squares
b) using every 5mm square
c) alternate 2.5mm squares
d) every 2.5mm square

on 5mm ($\frac{1}{4}$in.) squares, c and d on 2.5mm ($\frac{1}{8}$in.). Using alternate
squares where you can mark pinholes on intersections (as in a and
c) is obviously more accurate than placing a pinhole by 'eye' in the
middle of a square (b and d), however you may find larger squares
less confusing.

2. Most torchon patterns can be rearranged for mats, edgings,
insertions, etc.

3. The use of isometric (triangular) graph paper allows 6-sided
motifs to be produced. For example Fig. 70d which is worked on
Pricking 23 in the same way as the square.

In both Fig. 70c and Fig. 70d the workers for the fans were Fils à
Dentelles, remaining prs Gutterman metallic.

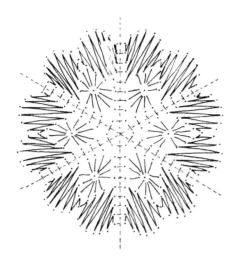

Bookworm (Fig. 74, Pricking 24)

A common feature of torchon edgings and insertions is the trail –
this is a zigzag band of w. or ½st. The trail may be continuous or
broken into sections. The 'worm' part of this bookmark is a
continuous w.st. trail. On either side are spiders, small sections of
½st. ground and standard footsides.

Use No. 8 coton perle, or No. 20 crochet cotton. Wind 14 prs in
1 colour plus 1 pr in a contrast (these will be wks for the trail).
Hang prs temporarily on *A* and *B*. The contrast (wks) should be
the 1st pr at *A*, with these and a pr from *B* work w.st., pin at 1,
w.st. Then work from side to side in w.st., bringing in prs at each
of pins 2–6.

Use passive prs (from 1 and 3) to work a square tally for the eye
(Fig. 73), support this with 2 pins, while the rest of the head is
worked.

Continue in w.st. bringing in new prs at 7, 8 and 10, and leaving
out prs at 9, 10, 11 and 12. At pin 13 no pr is taken in and no pr left
out – this is known as a *blind pin* (26 and 39 are also blind pins).

Work the 1st footside pin, at 14, with the pr from 10 and 2 prs
from *A*. Bring in the final 3 prs on the right with ½st., pin at 17, ½st,
and a footside pin at 18. Work a spider on the right noting that 2
of the legs will pass through the passives to/from the footside
pins. Work the next section of the trail (pins 22–27) before
working the spider, footside, etc on the left. Alternate trail and
spider until work reaches *X*.

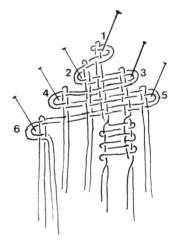

Fig. 73. Start of bookworm,
with tally worked for the eye

Finishing

Bring 3 prs from the edge into the trail at X, and threads from the right into the trail after Y – this makes the trail very thick so discard 1 pr of passives on every row (by turning the bobbins to the back of the pillow) until 4 prs remain. Work a short plait with these (from Z), tie and cut off as a tassel. Cut discarded threads close to the trail.

Pricking 24. Bookworm

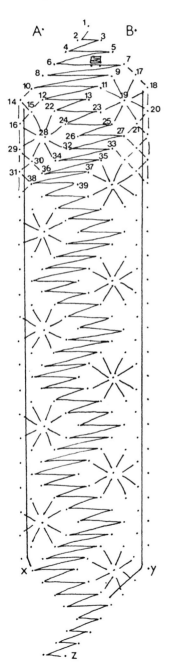

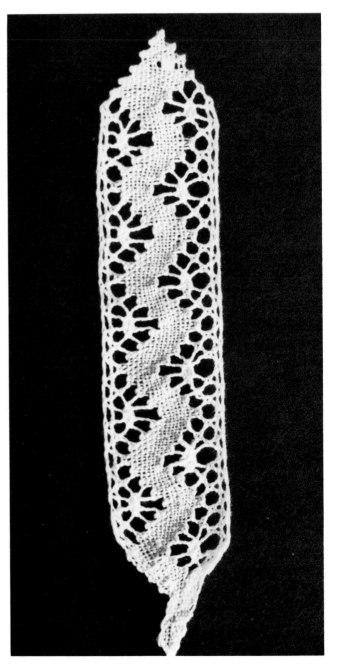

Fig. 74. Bookworm

Variations

1. Omit top and bottom of pricking and use the basic pattern as an insertion – you may want to add a row of pins on the left, or take one from the right, to make the 2 sides the same. The trail should be started with 2 prs on each of 26 and 27 and 2 prs on an extra pin stuck through the trail between these pins.

2. Replace spiders on 1 side, or both, with ground stitches.

3. Use ½st. instead of w.st. for the trail – on a ½st. trail you cannot use contrast threads.

The corner illustrated in Fig. 75, Pricking 25, has a ½st. trail and was worked with 14 prs (i.e. without the right-hand pins of Pricking 24). Notice the 4 threads going one way along the trail, 5 threads going the other – this is usual in a ½st. trail.

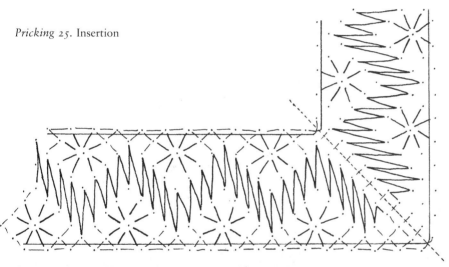

Pricking 25. Insertion

Fig. 75. Insertion with trail and spiders

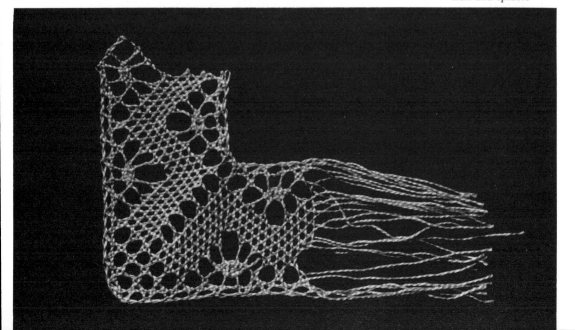

All the features of this edging have been worked in previous pieces. Work section by section as follows:

a) First part of w.st. trail, bringing in prs from *F* (see bookworm Fig. 73).

b) $\frac{1}{2}$st. diamond, bringing in 5 prs from *G* (see bookmark Fig. 36).

c) $\frac{1}{2}$st., pin, $\frac{1}{2}$st. ground (Fig. 31a), with standard footside (Fig. 44) and tally (Fig. 67) – this tally is worked at an angle since it fills the space between 4 pins rather than taking the place of one pin as in Fig. 66.

Finally 2 patterns requiring 20 or more prs of bobbins. One is for a traditional style edging, the other a modern 'fun' piece.

Wide Torchon Edging (Fig. 76, Pricking 26)

Twenty prs No. 8 coton perle. Start with 2 prs on each of *A* to *E*, remaining prs on support pins *F* and *G* – 5 prs on each.

Fig. 76. Wide torchon edging

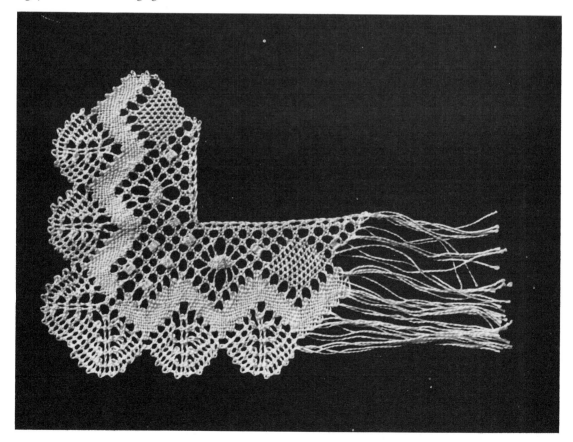

Pricking 26. Wide torchon edging, with diagram to show order of work

d) Second part of trail.
e) Fan (Figs. 27 and 28).
f) Trail.
g) Spider (Fig. 38b).
h) Ground, footside and tally.
i) Trail.
j) Fan.

Variations

Fig. 30 shows the edging with a ½st. trail and w.st. diamond. The 'variations' sections after the other torchon pieces will offer you more possibilities.

Owl (Fig. 77, Pricking 27a)

Twenty-four prs No. 8 coton perle (you can manage with 20 prs if you finish one wing before starting the other).

Hang 2 prs at each of A–D, and remaining prs on support pins (E, F and G) to be brought in a pr at a time at ringed pinholes.

Toes: triangular tallies – start each with a w.st. then work as for a square tally. Work tallies from A and B then work ½st., pin, ½st. as far as pin 9 before working toes from C and D.

Body: ½st., pin, ½st. ground with central spider.

Wings: ½st. – work as for ½st. diamond. At each pin marked with a cross a pr is left out of the work.

Beak: work ½st., pin, ½st. at a, move these prs to the side; tw. prs from b and c 3 times, work a w.st. with them then tw. 3 times again; lift prs from a into the centre again and work a long triangular tally.

Head: ½st., pin, ½st.

Eyes: lines show position of prs, work a dbl – no pin – where they cross.

Finishing

If mounting on fabric, darn all ends into the background. Alternatively knot prs tightly and cut close (sealing knot with a spot of glue if required).

Variations

The best way of varying this motif is by varying the thread – choose yarn and size of pricking to decorate anything from a key-ring (machine embroidery thread on 1mm ($\frac{1}{32}$in.) squares) Pricking 27b, to a bag (DK wool on 10mm ($\frac{1}{2}$in.) squares).

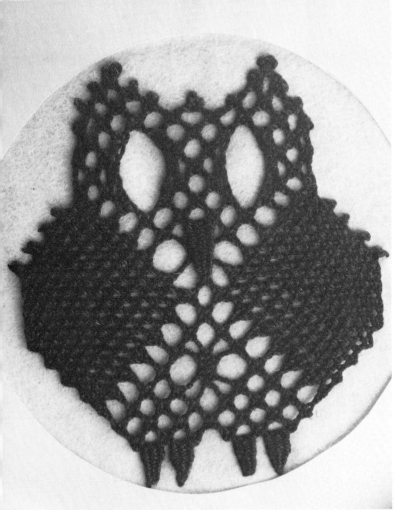

Fig. 77. Owl

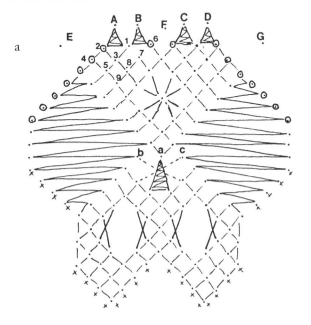

a

b

Pricking 27 Owl a) standard size b) miniature

6
What next?

Fig. 78. Varieties of lace:
a) Bedfordshire b) Bucks point,
worked by Sandra Staughair
from a Luton museum pricking
c) Honiton, worked by Susan
Roberts from one of Elsie
Luxton's patterns d) Bruges

The lace detailed in this book has been either torchon or braid lace, some of it traditional in form (e.g. half stitch fan edging, Fig. 42), some contemporary (e.g. Nessie, Fig. 60). This is only a fraction of the enormous range of bobbin lace varieties.

The basic stitches for all the laces are the same – it is the way the stitches are combined, plus a few specialised techniques and the correct choice of yarn that gives each style its distinctive quality.

Three traditional English laces, and one Belgian lace are illustrated in Fig. 78.

a) **Bedfordshire:** featuring plaits, picots and tallies.

b) **Bucks point:** worked with fine thread giving a very delicate net, with solid areas outlined by a thicker (gimp) thread.

c) **Honiton:** fine thread again – individual motifs are worked then joined and/or mounted on net.

d) **Bruges:** rather bold effect with scrolls and/or flowers and various fillings.

a) and b) are 'yard laces', i.e. the whole width of the lace is worked at once, requiring relatively large numbers of bobbins, but allowing long lengths to be worked. c) and d) are 'pieced laces', using fewer prs but requiring numerous sewings: a) needs nearly 50 prs, b) 30, while c) and d) require 16 prs or less.

Many books are now available containing both traditional and contemporary patterns, some with and some without detailed instructions. Try libraries and local bookshops or contact a lace supplier for his booklist (see short list of books and suppliers on pages 92–94).

Lacemaking classes are held in most areas of the UK – enquire at your library or local education department.

Whether you are learning on your own, or going to classes, try to get to a 'Lace Day'. There you will find lace suppliers with their wares, lacemakers of every ability (almost all prepared to share

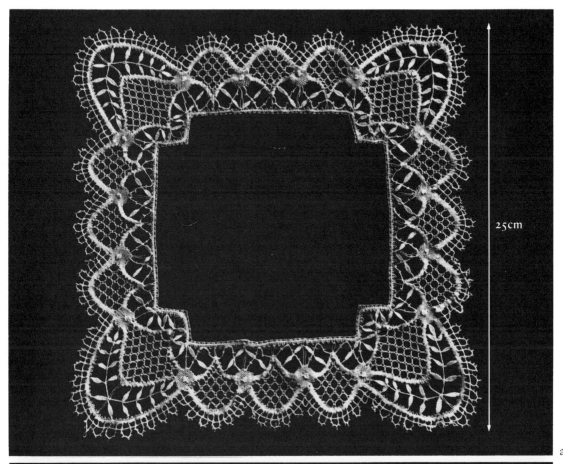

25cm

a

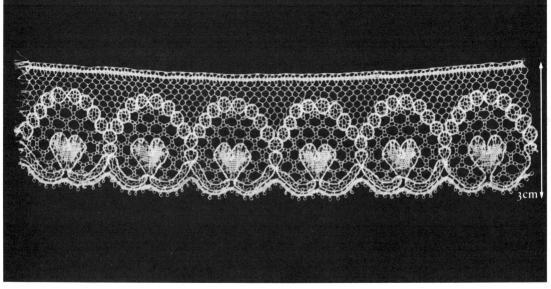

3cm

b

78c

78d

their experiences with you) and usually an interesting speaker or display to introduce you to some new aspect of the craft.

The Lace Guild exists to promote lacemaking in all its forms. Its quarterly magazine *Lace*, containing patterns, working instructions, suppliers' advertisements, information about lace days, exhibitions, etc, is available to all members. The Secretary, contacted at the Lace Guild Headquarters (The Hollies, 53 Audnam, Stourbridge, West Midlands, DY8 4AE) can give you more information and put you in touch with classes or other lacemakers in your area. (SAE please.)

Threads

Most threads sold for sewing, knitting, crochet, etc, can be used for lacemaking, however the following points are worth noting:

Yarns used for the samples in this book have been chosen for their availability and choice of colours – you should be able to find them in craft shops, department stores, etc. If you want to be more traditional then use an appropriate linen thread (e.g. Bockens linen No. 35 instead of No. 8 coton perle).

Threads should be chosen according to the proposed use of the finished piece – lace on an article of clothing, or table linen that will be subject to heavy wear and washing, should be made from a robust yarn such as crochet cotton or a good quality linen, while a picture that will be behind glass could be of any combination of threads.

Cotton and silk come in every colour of the rainbow. Linen is usually only available in white and neutral colours (but you could dye your own).

Some metallic yarns are inclined to break or kink badly when used for close stitches. The stretchiness of some synthetic yarns may make an even tension difficult.

Threads of apparently the same thickness will give different effects if one has a strong twist and another is only lightly twisted. Fig. 79 is, therefore, only a rough guide to the interchangeability of threads.

Pillows

As you make more lace you will probably find the need for another pillow. A selection is shown in Fig. 80. Each have their particular advantages and disadvantages.

Fig. 79. Threads: a) Coats Drima 120 b) DMC Brillante d'Alsace 50 c) DMC Brilliante d'Alsace 30 d) Bockens linen 90 e) Sylko 40 f) Bockens linen 50 g) Fils à Dentelles h) One strand of Anchor embroidery cotton i) DMC coton perle 12 j) Crochet cotton 50 k) Coton perle 8 l) Linen 35 m) Crochet cotton 20 n) Coton perle 5 o) Gutterman metallic p) DMC Fil Argent

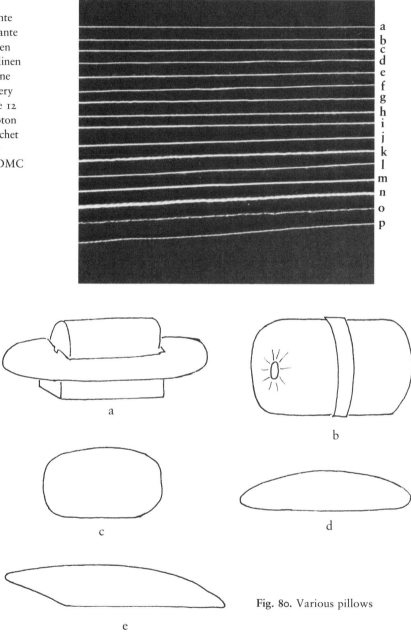

Fig. 80. Various pillows

a) Roller pillow – ideal for working long lengths.

b) Bolster – the traditional shape for working lengths.

c) 'Cheese' – for Honiton or other small motifs.

d) Domed polystyrene

e) Tightly packed straw on a rigid wood base } General purpose

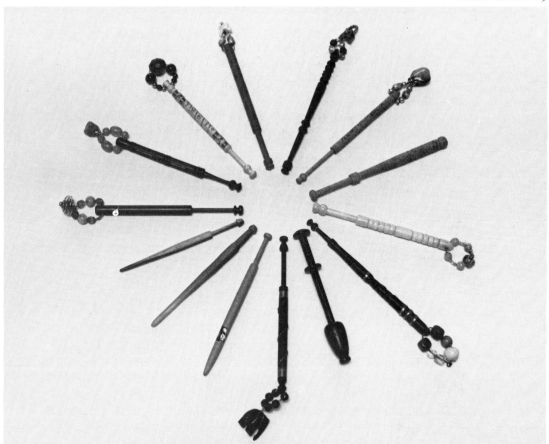

Bobbins

You are also likely to start collecting bobbins and will find that different shapes suit different types of lace, see Fig. 81 which includes two antique bobbins and a selection from the growing band of specialist bobbin makers.

Many of the bobbins will require spangling. The traditional spangle has seven or nine beads – a large bottom bead with smaller ones on each side. Old necklaces are a good source of beads for spangling – glass or ceramic beads are best, but lighter plastic, or even wood can be combined with heavier ones or small mementoes such as coins. Use good quality wire and position the join so the ends can be hidden inside beads or bobbin (Fig. 82).

Bobbins not in use should be kept in a padded box or a bobbin roll. The dimensions of the roll illustrated in Fig. 83 will allow a wound pr of standard, Bucks type (e.g. plastic), bobbins to be kept in each pocket – make suitable adjustments for larger or smaller bobbins.

Fig. 81. Bobbins in various styles and materials. Clockwise from the bottom: bead-bound bobbin with elephant spangle; three Honiton bobbins; Aluminium; Mother and Babe; Wire bound Christmas bobbin; two plastic bobbins; Northumbria Lacemakers bobbin; unspangled dowelling; antique bone; antique wood with pewter rings; Belgium

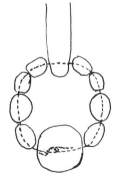

A crochet strip will keep bobbins in order on the pillow: with a size 2 or 2.5 crochet hook and an oddment of DK yarn (preferably light coloured and not too fluffy) make a foundation chain of about 30cms, then work one row double crochet, one row trebles and one row double crochet on this foundation and fasten off. Tuck bobbin heads into the holes. (Illustrated in the bottom corner of Fig. 1.)

Fig. 82. Bead spangle

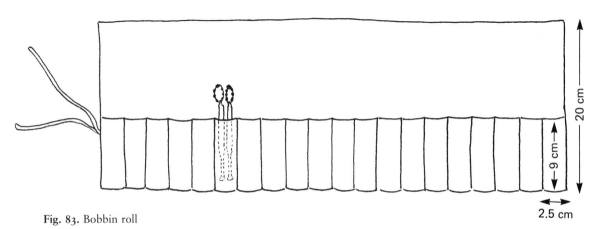

Fig. 83. Bobbin roll

Other Equipment

Tough plastic tracing film can be used instead of pricking card especially when trying out new patterns or working one-off pieces. The film is either placed over a paper pattern on the pillow, or the pattern is traced (or photocopied) directly onto the film which is then placed, ink-side down, over plain paper – when working in white thread use coloured paper (or tint with paint or ink). Pins will go through both film and paper without prior pricking. This type of pricking can be used several times on a firm pillow, but will not last as well as glazed card.

Some lacemakers find a bobbin winder useful – there are several types on the market, but most are expensive and hand winding is equally effective.

On the other hand there are two inexpensive items illustrated in Fig. 84 which may save temper and broken finger nails. a) at its simplest is a large nail in a block of wood – stand your reel of thread on this while you wind and you won't be chasing the reel across the floor. b) is a pin lifter, not necessary for 'yard laces', but very useful when pins have been pushed down to the pricking.

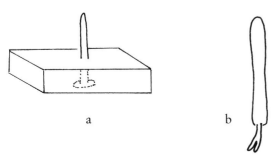

Fig. 84. a) spool holder b) pin lifter

a

b

Note book

A reference book with notes on each pattern you work will prove invaluable. Any notebook, pocket file, etc, would do, but the ideal is probably an A4 size ring binder containing coloured pages (e.g. paper sold 'by the lb') and transparent pockets. Keep in this any samples you work, along with the prickings, notes of the type of thread used, number of bobbins and any other information that might be useful in the future; e.g. source of pattern, date worked, special stitches or starting method, possible variations and ideas for applications.

Lacemaking Terms

The terms lacemakers use vary according to where and how they learned their lace. This may cause some confusion when you start to work from a new book (or with a different teacher), but a quick comparison of illustrations and text will usually sort out any problems. For example, what is here called a 'double' may be called 'cloth stitch and twist', 'workers' may be 'runners', etc.

I learned half stitch as tw., cr., but have changed, at least as far as teaching is concerned, to cr., tw. since this is the order used in the majority of English lace books. There is no difference in the finished effect – just whether the extra twist is needed when going from half stitch (or double) to whole stitch or vice versa.

Further Reading

Among the numerous lace books now available the following are
particularly suitable for relative beginners.

Bobbin Lacemaking, Pamela Nottingham, Batsford, London (Braids
and torchon)

Techniques of Bobbin Lace, Pamela Nottingham, Batsford, London
(Torchon, Beds, Bucks)

Manual of Hand-Made Bobbin Lacework, Margaret Maidment,
Batsford, London (Torchon, Beds, Bucks, honiton)

Technique of Honiton Lace, Elsie Luxton, Batsford, London
(Honiton)

Torchon Lace for Today, Jennifer Fisher, Dryad Press, London
(Torchon)

Bobbin Lace Braid, Gilian Dye, Batsford, London (Braids and a
little torchon)

Lacemaking: Point Ground, C.C. Channer, Dryad Press, London

Useful Addresses

UK

Alby Lace Centre
Cromer Road
Alby
Norwich
Norfolk

English Lace School
Honiton Court
Rockbeare
Nr Exeter
Devon

Frank Herring & Sons
27 High West Street
Dorchester
DT1 1UP
(Pillows, bobbins, winders)

Honiton Lace Shop
44 High Street
Honiton
Devon

D.J. Hornsby
149 High Street
Burton Latimer
Kettering
Northants
(All lacemaking requisites – mail order service)

Hepatica
82A Water Lane
Wilmslow
Cheshire

The Lace Guild
c/o The Hollies
53 Audnam
Stourbridge
West Midlands
DY8 4AE

Mace and Nairn
89 Crane Street
Salisbury
Wilts

B. Phillips
Pantglas
Cellan
Lampeter
Dyfed
(Bobbin maker)

Sebalace
76 Main Street
Addingham
Ilkley
West Yorks
LS29 0PL
(All lacemaking requisites)

A. Sells
49 Pedley Lane
Clifton
Shefford
Beds
*(All lacemaking requisites –
mail order service)*

D.H. Shaw
47 Zamor Crescent
Thurscroft
Rotherham
S. Yorks
(Bobbin maker)

C. & D. Springett
251 Hillmorton Road
Rugby
Warwicks
CV22 5BE
(Bobbin maker)

George White
Delaheys Cottage
Thistle Hill
Knaresborough
North Yorks
*(All lacemaking requisites
– mail order service)*

Christopher Williams
23 St. Leonards Road
Bournemouth
Dorset
BH8 8QL
(Old and new lace books)

USA

Berga–Ullman, Inc
P.O. Box 918
North Adams
Massachusetts O12 L17
(Materials and equipment)

Frederick J. Fawcett
129 South Street
Boston
Massachusetts 02130
*(Large selection of linen yarns and threads
up to size 140/2)*

International Old Laces
P.O. Box 1029
Westminster
Colorado 80030

Lacis
2990 Adeline Street
Berkeley
California 94703
*(All lacemaking requisites – mail order
service)*

Osma G. Tod Studio
319 Mendoza Avenue
Coral Gables
Florida 33134
*(Books, instructions, materials and
equipment)*

Robin and Russ Handweavers
533 N. Adams Street
McMinnville
Oregon 97128
(Books, materials and equipment)

The Unique and Antique Lace Cleaners
5926 Delmar Boulevard
St. Louis
Missouri 63112
(Professional lace cleaning and restoration)

Index